THE Healthy Mind Plan

THE Healthy Mind Plan

HOLISTIC TIPS TO BOOST YOUR MOOD

Edited by

EMMA VAN HINSBERGH

SIRIUS

SIRIUS

This edition published in 2023 by Sirius Publishing, a division of
Arcturus Publishing Limited,
26/27 Bickels Yard, 151–153 Bermondsey Street,
London SE1 3HA

Copyright © Arcturus Holdings Limited
Text © Kelsey Publishing Limited

ISBN: 978-1-3988-2045-6
AD008851UK

Printed in China

CONTENTS

INTRODUCTION

We all go through ups and downs during our lives, with challenges, pressures, responsibilities, expectations and new experiences having a huge impact on both our physical and mental health. No one feels fantastic all the time, but the good news is that making even the smallest changes to our lifestyle – for example, adding a little turmeric to your soup, setting aside a few minutes to meditate each day or jotting some notes in a gratitude journal – can make a huge difference in the long run, boosting our feelings of wellbeing and making us healthier and happier.

MIND AND BODY

Our mind and body are closely interconnected, so each naturally affects the other. This means that on the one hand our thoughts, feelings, beliefs and attitudes have an effect on the way our bodies function, and on the other hand the health of our bodies influences our mood and emotions. An example of the former might be the physical symptoms we experience when we are anxious or nervous – we may have shaking, sweaty hands, butterflies in our stomach or feelings of nausea. Or looking at it the

other way around, when we don't take good care of our body, such as when we haven't had a good night's sleep, haven't been eating healthily or haven't been exercising, we may feel depressed, lethargic or anxious. Our mind and body work together to make us whole, so looking after both is all part and parcel of our overall emotional and physical wellbeing.

IN THIS BOOK

In the pages that follow, we take the view that prevention is always better than cure – it's a good idea to look after our minds all the time, not just when we feel bad. So we provide simple tips that you can dip into whenever you feel the need for an instant pick-me-up or a reminder of how you can take back control and return to a healthier state of mind.

The chapters are organized as follows:

• We begin by presenting ways to calm your busy mind, beat anxiety and manage your worries.

• Next, we show how to harness your positivity by tapping into your inner joy and learning the art of forgiveness.

• Our chapter on relationships contains some intriguing questionnaires about attachment and bonding styles, because once you know how you bond with other people – whether you're a people pleaser, a peacemaker or an avoidant, for example – you can learn how to flourish within your own particular style.

• We then provide ideas for regaining balance and harmony in your life, from the Dutch practice of 'niksen' (doing nothing) to learning to be compassionate with yourself.

• The final chapter brings mind and body together, with techniques and nutritional ideas for optimizing health and wellbeing, plus a few great yoga exercises to help you release tension and unwind.

Enjoy your journey through the book – and we wish you well on your way to a happier, healthier and more harmonious you!

HOW TO DEAL WITH STRESS

Life can be hectic! From heavy workloads and office deadlines to school runs and busy household schedules, we're juggling so many balls, it's no wonder we feel the pressure sometimes. But what happens when it all gets on top of you? While it is natural to feel anxiety occasionally, if you feel it constantly, it can impact negatively on your life. The good news is that you don't need to be powerless in the face of your anxiety. You can learn to control it, and some of the ways to do that are actually quite simple...

WHY WORRY?

Try these quick tips to stop feeling so anxious.

For many of us, worrying is a part of life. We accept that anxiety is par for the course and that's that. However, recent research by wellbeing brand Healthspan has revealed that worrying isn't just part of life, it's taking over our lives, with women spending the equivalent of almost an entire month of the year worrying. In our books, that's one month too many.

Top concerns, among the study of 2,000 adults, were the health of loved ones, their family's safety and the needs of and caring for older parents. While these are completely legitimate worries, it becomes an issue when the amount of time you spend thinking and fretting about them begins to impact on your health.

In fact, 57 per cent of women surveyed admitted to neglecting their own health over fears about how it would affect their family, and 72 per cent dismissed their worrying health symptoms.

'We often hear people say, "I worry too much"', says Professor Margareta James, a psychologist at the Harley Street Wellbeing Clinic. 'Worrying affects not just our mental/emotional health but our physical health. It increases stress hormone levels and then it all kicks off from there. If it sticks around, something as small as a nagging concern in the back of your mind can affect your heart. It can make you more likely to have high blood pressure, a heart attack or a stroke.'

WORRYING IS NORMAL

Now before you begin to worry about how all your worrying is affecting your health, we're here to tell you it's completely normal to be concerned or anxious about things beyond your control. 'Worry is rooted in our biology,' says clinical psychologist Dr Aria (dr-aria. com), who specializes in the relationship between mental and physical health. 'The tendency for the human mind to worry about worst-case scenarios is actually an evolutionary hangover.'

So, if you've ever been referred to as a natural-born worrier, take heart in the fact that this is a perfectly normal attribute – especially among women.

'Because women's stress response is all about the tend-and-befriend, rather than the classic fight-or-flight, women will naturally worry about their loved ones,' says Dr Meg Arroll, a chartered psychologist. 'Managing all these competing demands often results in high levels of stress, which exhibits itself in behaviours such as comfort eating, poor sleep and anxiety. This is why self-care is so important.'

Try the following tips on how you can take control of your stress and worries, so that the next time you're hit with anxiety, you're ready.

Create 'good enough' reminders

You can use a phrase such as 'Iamgoodenough' as a password or as a background on your phone or tablet, or written on a post-it note on your bathroom mirror. This will help you give yourself a break, increasing self-compassion and reducing damaging perfectionism.

Fix your location device

When we worry, we tend to focus on events from the past or what might happen in the future. However, we cannot change the past or control the future – we can only act in the present. To fix yourself in the here and now, 'update' your internal location device by noting where your worries are situated – past, present and future – then focus on what can be achieved in the present moment.

Set yourself 'worry work'

Plan some time for your worries. Set a timer for 15 minutes, and during this time, worry your socks off! This will allow you to remove that background worry noise, so you can concentrate on daily tasks free from intrusive thoughts.

Tools to quieten a racing brain

The government-backed Good Thinking programme (good-thinking.uk) offers a range of tools and resources to help you manage stress and worry. Or try the mindfulness toolkit from Think Well Live Well (thinkwell-livewell.com), which includes a 5-minute quick stress buster.

Write down your worries

Try to break your worries down into parts, ranking them in order of importance. Work out a solution for each task and when to complete it. Plan a reward for achieving each goal.

Take up a hobby

Do something that brings you into the present moment through focusing on what you are doing. When you are painting, drawing or creating, you bring yourself into the present moment and the worries about the future quieten down.

Release endorphins

There are several ways in which you can release endorphins, which are our feel-good hormones. After a good laugh, for example, your heart rate and blood pressure decrease, leading to a lovely, relaxed feeling.

Another great ways to help reduce worry is to exercise. When you work out, this gets your heart pumping with feel-good endorphins flowing around your body.

Massage and meditation also stimulate endorphin release, as does eating foods like chocolate and chillies.

Going for a run is a great way to release endorphins and take your mind off your worries for a while.

CALM YOUR BUSY MIND

Try this seven-day plan to beat hyper-stimulation and find inner peace.

Do you often find yourself mindlessly scrolling through your phone? You're not alone. More than 96 per cent of Brits own a smartphone, and data show we feel anxious or stressed without it. There are other pleasures out there too: sugar, alcohol, shopping, TV. The world is full of stimulating activities that encourage the body to produce the feel-good chemical dopamine. But what if abstaining from these could help you find pleasure in simple things? Enter the dopamine fast...

Dopamine fasting is the latest craze to emerge from Silicon Valley in the US. Created by San Francisco psychologist Dr Cameron Sepah, it's about temporarily avoiding addictive behaviours such as social media scrolling. This avoidance is said to make the seemingly mundane, such as a walk in the woods, feel very pleasurable again. 'The primary purpose is to spend less time engaging in behaviours that have become problematic,' says Dr Sepah. 'The techniques are derived from Cognitive Behavioural Therapy (CBT), which is considered the gold standard treatment for impulse control disorders.' Dr Sepah adds that it's not about abstaining from enjoyment forever, but training yourself to regain control over impulsive actions. 'You needn't "do nothing" or meditate the whole time, unless you'd like to. Just engage in regular activities that reflect your values,' he says.

BREAKING COMPULSIVE BEHAVIOURS

Experts are sceptical, as dopamine is important to lots of everyday tasks. 'Dopamine is a neurotransmitter involved in many brain functions such as motor control and reward processing,' says Dr Ciara McCabe, associate professor of neuroscience at the University of Reading.

'Dopamine activity spikes when a new reward arrives, such as food or drugs. Interestingly, though, over time dopamine can predict when rewards are coming by learning the cues associated with the reward. This means dopamine then spikes more to the cue than to the reward itself.'

However, abstaining from a compulsive activity may decrease dopamine activity, and that could be healthy. 'If you find certain behaviours, such as looking at social media, problematic, or end up watching endless TV, reducing your engagement with the cues could help you stop,' she adds. 'For example, you can turn off autoplay on Netflix so you don't get cued into watching another episode.' And many clinicians argue that the benefits go beyond dopamine changes. 'It will also encourage quality interaction with people,' says Natalia Ramsden, founder of brain optimization clinic SOFOS Associates (sofosassociates. com). 'It will allow mental rest and, importantly, promote quality sleep.'

Dopamine fasting involves abstaining from social media, online gaming and listening to music, which allows you time to engage in healthy interactions.

YOUR SEVEN-DAY DOPAMINE FASTING PLAN

WANT TO DIP into the dopamine fasting trend? There are no hard rules. Dr Sepah recommends avoiding all problematic activities – whether eating fast food, using the internet or watching TV – for a block of time and increasing your 'fasting' of these things over time, starting with 1–4 hours per day and building up to one weekend per year.

Try out the plan below, but also feel free to include your own ideas, depending on your particular dopamine fixes.

DAY 1 – Cut out coffee Recreational drugs, including caffeine, are off the cards during a dopamine fast. Avoid them in the 4 hours leading up to bedtime to enjoy the added health benefit of better sleep.

DAY 2 – Take a tech break Give your brain a break from constantly scrolling through social media, binge-watching television or playing computer games by having a digital detox for the last 4 hours of the day. Switch your phone off and put it out of sight. Read a book instead.

DAY 3 – So long, sugar! Dr Sepah suggests either doing intermittent fasting or simply banishing unhealthy foods altogether. Avoid highly processed fodder such as sugary or salty snacks for the whole day.

DAY 4 – Start a shopping ban Whether online or on the high street, give shopping the heave-ho for the rest of the week. Dr Sepah likens shopping to gambling, because it involves spending money to feel better.

DAY 5 – Ditch Friday drinks Just like caffeinated beverages, alcohol can be considered a recreational drug. Unwind from the working week with a non-alcoholic bevvy, of which there are plenty these days!

DAY 6 – Be mindful of music Some people on a dopamine fast choose not to listen to music because it can elicit arousing emotions. So try spending your Saturday doing some quiet exercise, creative writing or art.

DAY 7 – Spend time alone Natalia says many people fast from social activities, so spend time alone today. Try doing one of the health-giving activities Dr Sepah recommends, such as reading, writing, cooking or exercising.

HOW TO FEEL CALMER

Reducing your stress levels can help you to feel calmer and happier, and there are plenty of ways to take back control.

Not only can stress make you look visibly older, it can also increase your risk of developing a serious disease. Chronic stress (stress over a prolonged period of time) can increase your risk of cancer, lung disease and even liver disease if you are using alcohol to help you unwind. Stress can also affect our moods. Neuroscientists at New York University found that even mild stress levels can affect our emotions and make us more likely to fly off the handle. Stress can damage your heart, too. Your heart rate increases when you're stressed, forcing your heart to work harder, and it also increases your blood pressure. Clearly there are many good reasons to combat stress, but if you can't completely remove it from your life, there are ways you can change your lifestyle so that you can cope with it better. Here are some top tips to help you...

Find something you love
Find an activity or a hobby that brings you pleasure, and do it as much as you can. Taking time out from the source of your stress now and then will help you unwind and give you more resilience to cope with daily problems and stresses.

Sort out your diet

Make simple yet sustainable changes to your diet. Some foods contain ingredients that will actually help you calm down. Oily fish, chicken, turkey, wholegrains, berries and nuts are all good choices. However, if you're trying to lose weight, consume nuts only in moderation, as they are also high in calories.

Reduce caffeine and sugar

Too much sugar will lead to weight gain, which can make you more stressed if you're unhappy with your figure. But caffeine, sugar, chocolate and pastries can also contribute to increased stress. Sugar and caffeine will give you a temporary high, but you will end up with a crash in energy levels, which will affect your mood.

Eat lots of antioxidants

For a stress-free diet, consume plenty of complex carbohydrates, such as wholegrain bread and pasta, foods high in vitamin A such as oranges, foods high in magnesium like spinach, soybeans or salmon, and antioxidant-rich black and green tea.

Get a pet (or stroke one!)

Research indicates that those with animals are less likely to suffer from depression than those without. Dog and cat owners are reported to have lower blood pressure in stressful situations than those without animals, and it's thought that stroking a cat can reduce your blood pressure by up to 30 per cent! Plus, research shows that pet owners over the age of 65 make 30 per cent fewer visits to the GP than those without pets.

Get fit

Taking regular exercise and getting fit will reduce your stress levels, because exercise releases feel-good endorphins. You may find it a challenge to exercise after a stressful day, but that's the time when you

Green tea is a calming alternative to ordinary tea or coffee. It is high in the amino acid L-theanine, which may lower anxiety.

will benefit most. Usually, fatigue caused by stress is more mental than physical, so even if you don't feel like it, vow to exercise for 20 minutes. At the end of the 20 minutes, you'll want to do more!

Switch off your brain at night

To be at your most resilient, you need to rest well at night. If you have trouble sleeping, try having a warm drink and reading a fictional (non-stressful) book before you turn off the lights. Avoid watching late-night TV with graphic or violent scenes and keep technology out of the bedroom so that you're not tempted to check emails or do some work.

Get enough sleep

Most of us need between 6 and 8 hours of sleep per night, but some people may need more than that. Work out how much you need to function well. If you struggle to drop off at night and your mind is constantly buzzing, try some meditation before you go to bed. Try using Calm (www.calm.com), an app that provides guided meditations with different themes, including one that focuses on releasing anxiety.

Set some boundaries

'Stress can be caused by too much work, leaving you feeling that the balance isn't where you'd like it to be,' says life coach Jeff Archer, owner of corporate wellbeing consultancy The Tonic (www.the-tonic.com). 'You'll find it harder to maintain balance in your routine if you're not clear what good balance looks like, so be diligent in planning and making time for the things you enjoy and that nourish your overall success.' Don't be afraid to make your expectations clear, which may sometimes mean saying 'no'.

Keep a journal

Even if you don't write something every day, just write a few of your thoughts down – especially what's been worrying you – whenever you have time. This can be quite therapeutic.

Writing about your feelings and worries is a good way to process your daily thoughts and emotions. You might also try making a list, writing a poem or inventing a story with you as the main character.

BEAT ANXIETY AND FIND CALM

Beyond feelings of agitation or worry, anxiety is a complex disorder that can tip over into excessive unease, panic and compulsive behaviour.

Approximately eight million people in the UK experience some form of anxiety, and it is considered one of the most common psychiatric disorders. It is perfectly normal to feel fearful at times but anxiety is not the same as feeling stressed, which is a natural response to precarious or challenging times. Anxiety is a condition that persists, whether the cause of it is clear to you or not.

A PHYSICAL REACTION

When we are scared, the body's fight-or-flight response, controlled by our sympathetic nervous system, is activated. The sympathetic nervous system is one part of the autonomic nervous system. The other is the parasympathetic nervous system, which works to slow down and relax the body's stress response. The good news is that we can learn to trigger our parasympathetic nervous system to reduce feelings of anxiety, lift our mood, strengthen our immune system and reduce our blood pressure. Sam Owen, author of *Anxiety Free: How to Trust Yourself and Feel Calm*, goes one step further and suggests we might even be able to reframe anxiety as a benign force, guiding us towards our goals, health, happiness and survival. 'Anxiety is both a mental and physical health feedback loop,'

DO YOU HAVE ANXIETY?

A checklist of common symptoms:

- Restlessness or inability to sit still.
- Headaches, backache and other aches and pains.
- Shortness of breath.
- A fast, thumping or irregular heartbeat.
- Sweating or feeling hot.
- Sleeping problems.
- Grinding your teeth, especially at night.
- Nausea.
- Needing the toilet more or less often.
- Changes in your sex drive.
- Panic attacks.

Try the NHS mood self-assessment at nhs.uk/conditions/stress-anxiety-depression/mood-self-assessment (it asks the questions GPs ask to diagnose anxiety or depression). For more resources, go to mind.org.uk.

she explains. 'It exists because your brain is trying to alert you to a threat to your mental or physical wellbeing or survival. Anxiety is just our brain's way of trying to keep us alive and well.'

There are myriad self-help practices and techniques at our fingertips and practically a library of books we can use to discover ways of combatting anxiety and staying mentally well. However, some people struggling with an anxiety disorder may feel plagued by irrational fear and worry that they are unable to cope.

Even when there are no obvious external factors, sufferers of anxiety can experience some or all of the physical and emotional symptoms of anxiety, and these feelings can be overwhelming, stopping us from functioning or making us behave in unusual ways.

SALT ON THE WOUND

Those who do not suffer from anxiety may find overwhelming anxiety in others difficult to understand. Sufferers may feel ashamed of our emotional state and hide how we feel, which can isolate us further and keep us trapped in a downward spiral. 'Patients often talk of being told to "stop worrying", "think positively" or "stop overthinking things". These sorts of attitudes lead to people with anxiety concealing how they feel and not asking for the support they need and deserve,' says NHS consultant psychiatrist Muffazal Rawala. 'Although it is important to address our negative thoughts, anxiety is an illness from which people cannot "snap out of" – and evidence-based pharmacological and psychological treatments can be sought to alleviate the symptoms and offer recovery.' Whether our anxiety is a long-term condition that we have to manage on an ongoing basis, a recent response to the coronavirus pandemic or another event or change in our lives, it is a real condition to be taken

WHAT KIND OF ANXIETY DO YOU HAVE?

CLINICAL HYPNOTHERAPIST and nutritionist Chloe Brotheridge, who specializes in treating people with severe anxiety, outlines the main types of anxiety below.

Generalized anxiety disorder (GAD)

This can be nervousness, fear or worry. 'Worrying is one of the major symptoms of GAD – not being able to stop worrying, and worrying about many different things,' says Brotheridge. Physical manifestations are very common. 'Unless they have had anxiety, people don't realize how physical it is. GAD might mean a nervous stomach and a need to go to the toilet more frequently, shaking, experiencing surges of adrenaline and nervous energy in your body, or that you can't keep still, sweating, problems with sleep, fidgeting and an inability to concentrate.'

Panic attacks

For many of us, panic attacks are a physical symptom. 'During a panic attack, we can feel as if we are having a heart attack. Many people end up in A&E because they think they are dying,' says Brotheridge.

Post-traumatic stress disorder (PTSD)

This develops after being involved in, or witnessing, traumatic events. According to the mental health charity Mind, common symptoms include vivid flashbacks or feeling like the trauma is happening again, intrusive thoughts or images, nightmares, intense distress at real or symbolic reminders of the trauma, and physical sensations such as pain, sweating, nausea and trembling.

Obsessive-compulsive disorder (OCD)

This usually causes a particular pattern of thoughts and behaviour. Obsessive, unwanted, intrusive and distressing thoughts, images or compulsive urges repeatedly enter the mind, and we feel driven to perform certain acts or mental routines as we seek calm.

Social anxiety

This is more than shyness. 'Social anxiety is actually a fear of judgement by other people. It can hold us back from talking to and meeting others. We might get nervous before meeting people, shaky, avoid social situations and feel intense fear. Social anxiety isn't necessarily a fear of crowds or people that we know, it's usually a fear of judgement that is at the root of it,' says Brotheridge.

seriously, and there is help and support available. With the right tools, we can make ourselves feel better and, if self-help methods are insufficient in the short or long term, we must seek professional assistance.

SEVEN WAYS TO COMBAT ANXIETY

We are not powerless in our fight against anxiety. These effective, proven self-help strategies can help us take back control and feel stronger.

1. Be specific

For many of us, anxiety is a nameless dread, so it's important to investigate what's triggering our fears, says Owen. Ask: Is it real or imagined? Is it self-generated anxiety from our thoughts, or repetitive negative thinking about ourselves and our self-image? Or is our behaviour actually causing the problem? Are we behaving in line with our authentic self? Are we overloaded and taking on too many tasks, or processing too much information? Or is the cause externally generated? Maybe our anxiety stems from negative relationships or a problem at work. After identifying the cause, make a plan to overcome the threat: create self-serving positive thoughts that soothe or eliminate anxiety in

the moment; build positive relationships and prune negatives ones; take proper self-care; and create simple, fun strategies that calm. Ask goal-focused, solution-focused, empowering questions – for example, what would make me feel less anxious and more optimistic about my career? 'Once you know what is causing your anxiety, you can take action to tackle it,' says Owen.

Try this: Owen suggests several strategies, including simple, easy-to-adopt ones such as a social media diet and learning how to breathe for a peaceful mind (inhale calm for a count of three, hold for three and exhale for three, breathing out tension). Write down a couple of associated specific goals, such as: spend only one hour on social media today. You can also rewire your brain to reduce anxiety by learning new things, taking some form of exercise every day and building self-care into your daily routine.

2. Beware perfectionism

Trying to do everything perfectly is a common trigger for anxiety. 'The internet offers a bottomless pit of people with whom to compare ourselves, and can be harmful for anyone with low self-esteem. It's tempting to go looking for inspiration and, after scrolling for hours, end up feeling like a failure. The pressure of perceived perfection, whether in our careers, home, relationships or appearance, is overwhelming for many of us. The frustrating thing is that, most of the time, the pressure to be perfect is self-inflicted and doesn't need to be there,' says Fiona Thomas, author of *Depression in a Digital Age: The Highs and Lows of Perfectionism*. Starting to notice the thoughts that trigger our perfectionism can help us cultivate new ways of thinking. If we uncover that the pressure for perfectionism is fuelling our anxiety, we can use self-awareness to begin to unpick the problem and try to manage and understand our feelings.

Try this: 'Tune in to the narrative you've written for yourself and listen to the little voice in your head. It can be difficult at first, so start with affirmations and think about how your mind responds to them. Try repeating the phrase, "I don't have to be perfect all the time" and see how you feel. Does your mind contradict that statement? Do you instantly want to believe that perfection is the only option?' asks Thomas. 'Another useful affirmation is: "I trust that whatever I do today is enough". It's about being at peace with how things unfold. It doesn't mean giving up and not trying in life but accepting that perfection doesn't exist and chasing it is pointless.'

3. Heal yourself

A recent study found that hatha yoga – designed to align and calm mind, body and spirit – brought positive results for people with anxiety. A previous study demonstrated that hatha yoga reduced anxiety more than walking. Researchers suggest this is due to increased levels of the brain chemical gamma-aminobutyric acid (GABA) in those who practise yoga. GABA tends to be lower in people with anxiety and mood disorders. 'Restorative yoga takes the stillness at the heart of the practice and puts it centre stage. It takes us from the fight-or-flight mode of our stressful lives and allows us to settle into the parasympathetic nervous system where we might find calm. It is ideal for those with anxiety, because its long-held and deeply felt poses boost the immune system and calm the mind,' explains Naomi Annand, yoga teacher and author of *Yoga: A Manual for Life*.

Try this: 'My favourite restorative pose, which I use every day, is viparita karani – legs up the wall, resting my hands on my belly and tuning in to my breath,' says Annand.

4. Challenge your fears

Cognitive behavioural therapy (CBT) is a talking therapy that focuses on how our thoughts, beliefs and attitudes affect our feelings and behaviour, and teaches us coping skills for dealing with problems. It combines cognitive therapy (examining what we think) and behaviour therapy (examining what we do), and research shows that is highly effective in treating anxiety.

Try this: 'Write a list of all the things that frighten you,' says Susan Smith, psychotherapist, clinical hypnotherapist and co-author of *I Just Want to be Happy*. Then challenge each one. 'Look at every point and ask yourself: 'Is it true?' Reply honestly. If it's true, what can you do to change the situation? Write down even the tiniest thing to make a small shift. 'The power to change is within us. Even if you're in the worst possible situation, start to make an escape plan. Write down the steps you need to take to get out of the job, relationship or situation. 'When you write things down, you are beginning to make a commitment to yourself to make your life better and become empowered.' You can find out more about CBT and where to get treatment at mind.org.uk and thestresshacker.com.

5. Get creative

Art therapy is an effective way to tackle anxiety. In creating art, we are able to focus on our perceptions, imagination and feelings. An art therapist will encourage you to express your inner world, and mindful art therapy has been proven to reduce anxiety.

Try this: 'Art therapy is a simple way to externalize your anxiety and observe it instead of feeling controlled by it,' says Smith. 'With your non-dominant hand, draw your anxiety. Don't worry about what your drawing looks like – no one will see it. Next, with either hand, draw a picture that represents how it would feel if you could shrink and contain your anxiety. Add drawings of what you think your diminished fear would look like.'

6. Talk to someone

Research published in *The Lancet Psychiatry* suggests that talking therapy with someone with no vested interest can be a more successful treatment than prescription drugs, and have longer lasting effects too. 'We could all do with therapy,' says Brotheridge. 'Although opening up to loved ones can ease the burden of isolation, it can be useful to talk to someone who won't judge you, and where you won't feel judged.'

Try this: Talking therapy can provide a safe space to uncover a discourse around your anxiety, 'even though it might sometimes seem overwhelming or scary to begin with,' notes Brotheridge. 'Ask your GP what they recommend and whether they can put you on a waiting list to see a psychotherapist or counsellor,' she urges.

7. Take a mindful shower

Neuropsychiatrist Jeffrey Schwartz of the University of California studied and treated a group of OCD sufferers, who showed unusually high fear reactions. A Buddhist, Schwartz was intriguedby therapeutic mindfulness, in which you stand outside your mind, observing thoughts and feelings as if they are happening to someone else. Working with patients with moderate to severe OCD, Schwartz showed them scans of their brains overreacting. He taught them to use mindfulness to focus on the idea that their compulsions were just misfiring brain circuitry; they didn't need to act and were simply witnessing the arrival of an obsessive thought. Out of 18 patients, 12 stopped their OCD behaviour. Schwartz found that their brains had changed structurally and concluded that the brain that observes itself changes itself.

Try this: 'Anxiety is based in past memories or projected worries of the future, it has nowhere to go when you are in the present,' says Nick Scaramanga of the Zenways mindfulness programme. 'Meditation is brilliant but you can do anything mindfully. Try creating a morning routine where you mindfully get out of bed, brush your teeth and have a shower. Slow everything down, notice the air on your skin, the water swirling around your toes, the sounds and sensations. Notice the thoughts that come and go – the trick is not to get hooked by them, but simply observe them.'

MAJOR IRRITANT

Do you find yourself getting irritated frequently? Here's how to get over it...

Selfish children, noisy commuters, loud music. Do you often find yourself being driven mad by pesky annoyances? 'Irritation is a state of feeling annoyed or impatient,' says psychologist David Cohen, author of *What Bugs You?* – a study of irritation and its causes. 'It's a diluted form of anger that tends to be driven by lots of little things and rarely coalesces around a single big thing, the way anger does.'

Irritation is more common than anger and yet less talked about. There is a lot of literature about anger and hardly any about irritation. Most of us knowhow to step back from anger but find ourselves succumbing quite easily to irritation. 'There are two typical responses to irritation,' says Michael Sinclair, a consultant psychologist at City Psychology Group and author of *The Little ACT Workbook: An Introduction to Acceptance and Commitment Therapy.* 'We tend to either keep it to ourselves and allow it to affect us or we flip and act on it.' Both responses are problematic. 'If you keep it to yourself, you tend to start ruminating and it begins to become about you rather than something external. But if you react impulsively to the irritant, you can exacerbate the situation and make it worse.'

So what's going on here? Why do we get irritated and what's the point of it, if it just increases tension all round? Evolutionary help or hindrance? 'All emotions have a function,' says Sinclair. 'Irritation raises our awareness of a given situation, alerting us to the fact that we might have to do something about it. It's an evolutionary function and designed to keep us safe in a threatening world. The trouble is that our typical responses tend to exacerbate the situation, our stress hormones leap into action, we go into fight-or-flight mode and the tension increases.'

So, how do we use irritation the right way? Sinclair prescribes practising diffusion, a process of paying attention to thoughts and recognizing that they are just things going on in our mind. Let it linger or let it go? 'Don't allow the emotion to control your mind and body. Step back from it. Ask yourself if you want to be a person who lets irritants fester, an angry person, or if you want to be an assertive but kind person, or even a more tolerant person. When we have awareness of our emotions, we can make better choices about how to respond.'

'Irritation tends to be triggered by a feeling of vulnerability,' says Sinclair. 'This often stems from low self-esteem or follows a series of difficult life events. When you recognize that you are feeling vulnerable to things that are beyond your control, you need to treat yourself as a friend may treat you. Be kind to yourself. Remind yourself that it's not personal. Give yourself a hug.'

PUT THOSE BUGBEARS TO BED

PSYCHOLOGIST Michael Sinclair recommends Acceptance and Commitment Therapy (ACT), a three-step process designed to deal with problematic emotions.

1. **Diffusion.** Pay attention to your thoughts and recognize that they are just thoughts and not anything that anyone is doing to you. Yes, there may be an external irritant but your reaction to it is yours – and you can modify how you react.
2. **Distance.** Describe your irritation. Give it shape, colour and form, and in doing so create a sense of distance between yourself and the emotion. This will also enable you to make wiser choices about how you deal with it.
3. **Kindness.** Be kind to yourself. Acknowledge that something is irritating you and try to soothe yourself the way you might soothe someone else. Breathe slowly or give yourself a hug; both release oxytocin, which promotes feelings of wellbeing.

MANAGE YOUR WORRIES

There are several ways in which you can manage your 'worry time'. Think about how you might get help when you need it, and try the following techniques.

A SHOULDER TO LEAN ON

When you need support, find the courage to ask for help. When people are going through difficult times, friends often feel helpless. Asking for help doesn't mean you are needy, incapable or weak. How would you feel if someone you cared about was struggling and you didn't know because they didn't tell you? How would you feel if a friend asked for your assistance? Make a list of people who could get you through a challenging time in different ways:

- People who have experienced a similar situation.
- People who have specific skills that could help.
- People who are great listeners.
- People who will give you a 'kick in the pants' if needed.
- People who lift your spirits and make you laugh.
- People who are good at problem-solving.
- People who are great organizers.
- People who can connect you to others who might help.

Think about what an amazing support network you could create and how good your friends will feel knowing they are doing something to help you.

REDUCE WORRY AND RUMINATION

Rumination is the tendency to keep thinking about things you can't change, to worry about something that has happened or might happen and to replay events in your mind, wondering whether you could have done them differently.

If you are prone to rumination, try the following method to reduce it. Set aside a specific time every day to worry. Allow only 15 minutes a day. Decide when and where you are going to do it. Postpone any worrying until the allocated worry period, when you can worry as much as you like — but you must stop after 15 minutes.

START A GRATITUDE JOURNAL

It is easy to get stuck focusing on the negatives in life, particularly when you are experiencing loss and grief brought about by change. To redress the balance, buy a journal and list all the things you are grateful for in life. If you make gratitude a regular habit, you will shift your perspective and you are likely to:

- Realize what is important to you.
- Appreciate what you have going for you.
- Appreciate other people more.
- Feel a greater sense of calm.

HOW TO HARNESS POSITIVITY

The world deals us some knocks sometimes, and negative emotions such as grief and sadness are part of the great rollercoaster of life. But if you can find a way to address these emotions, you'll find yourself in a much happier, more harmonious place. This chapter shows how to do just that.

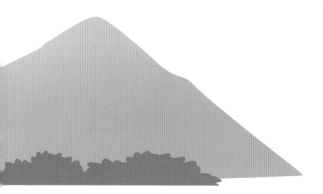

FIND YOUR INNER JOY

Here's how to tap into your inner joy to bring more harmony into your life...

Why is it that joy is an emotion that we rarely acknowledge, let alone prioritize? We often believe that joy is childish a bit silly or superficial, especially because it's an emotion that lives in small moments that are easily overlooked. In fact, research indicates that joyful moments are really powerful. Joy can improve our performance at work as well as change the way we interact with others, and it can make us 12 per cent more productive because it improves our working memory, the part of the brain we use for complex tasks during which we need to focus.

According to Ingrid Fetell Lee, author of *Joyful: The Surprising Power of Ordinary Things to Create Extraordinary Happiness*, the most counterintuitive behaviour people adopt concerning joy is the tendency to postpone it, particularly when we're going through challenging times. 'Typically we might say: "I won't go out for dinner tonight I'll stay at home and work on the project that's stressing me out. I can have fun next week when it's all over." The truth is that if we allow ourselves to experience joy during difficult times, it helps us to combat stress. Joy allows us to develop more resilience and find more meaning and purpose in the midst of challenges,' she says.

Research by psychologist Barbara Fredrickson reveals that if you allow yourself to experience small moments of joy, such as buying yourself a bag of sweets, you will be more likely to see the bigger picture when solving complex problems, as well as coming up with creative solutions.

CAN YOU FEEL IT RIGHT NOW?

Another immediate issue when it comes to creating more joy is that it's an emotion that is frequently used interchangeably with happiness, even though there are distinct differences between the two. 'Happiness is a broad evaluation about how we feel about our life over time and it encompasses a complex range of elements,' explains Fetell Lee. 'At times, the concept of happiness can feel quite vague. If someone were to ask you how happy you are right now, on a scale of one to 10, you would probably struggle to come up with an answer. You would have to ask yourself – how do I feel about my work, health, family and relationships?' Joy, on the other hand, can be defined as an intense, momentary experience of positive emotion. 'We can measure joy through direct physical expression – laughter; a feeling of wanting to jump up and down,' says Fetell Lee. 'It differs for everyone but what's important is to start to pay attention to what it feels like in the body. It creates a physical reaction just as, for example, we can identify when we're anxious because we have butterflies in our stomach and clammy hands. The more we notice that joy is a physiological experience, the more we can start to catch hold of those moments in our day.'

INSTANT JOY STRATEGIES

TRY THESE TIPS to generate more joy in your life:

Become a joy detective
Fetell Lee observes that while the concept of the 'downward mood spiral' has been well documented, people often forget that you can develop an upward spiral too. We are programmed with a negativity bias – to pay attention to negative stimuli because early humans needed to be hyper-vigilant for threats such as marauding lions in order to survive. The more we pay attention to negative things, the more we notice them. But the same is true for positive stimuli. 'It takes a little effort but it's well worth doing,' says Fetell Lee. 'Start by keeping a joy journal to note down all the times during a given day that you experienced joy. What was happening? Who were you with and what sensory experiences were present? Record the details; the more specific, the better. If you get stuck in your head, a great question to ask – suggested to me by a six-year-old child – is: What was the silliest thing that happened to me today? That one question can reframe everything.'

Bubbles and rainbows!
Although we're forever being told that experiences rather than possessions are the root to happiness, Fetell Lee believes that is not

the whole story. Certain things seem to bring joy to people the world over: bubbles in the bath and blown into the sky, rainbows, confetti, hot air balloons, ice cream cones with sprinkles and maybe a flaky chocolate... There are unifying patterns – round shapes, bright colours and small objects repeated many times, such as polka dots and jelly beans. It sounds whimsical, but there is scientific evidence to back it up. Studies reveal that the human brain responds more positively to curved shapes than angular ones, and also towards bright berry hues (because we needed to pay attention to those plants that were a source of food). Fetell Lee suggests experimenting by introducing more of these ingredients into your daily life.

Adopt a morning gratitude practice

'If you're going to pick one practice to create a more joyful mindset, make it gratitude,' according to life coach Veronica Moreno. 'The best time to do this is first thing in the morning because we know that how we start our day sets the tone for what follows. You can meditate on gratitude, journal about it or even make a playlist to put you back in touch with what you're most grateful for in your life,' she advises.

'Start small... Maybe appreciate a colleague for their sense of humour, instead of focusing on what you may dislike about them. But it's not just about thinking pleasant thoughts – express your gratitude too. Think about small things you can do, like bringing chocolate into the office as an appreciative gesture for the great team you work alongside. Change starts with making a choice about where to focus your energy.

Schedule a weekly 'joy date'

Schedule a joy date in the same way as Julia Cameron, writer of *The Artist's Way*, prescribes an artist's date. 'Book time in your diary for a joyful activity,' says Moreno. 'It doesn't have to be ambitious; it could be a walk in the park, reading a book you love or journalling. Give yourself permission to make joy a priority in your life.' Moreno believes joy is crucially important to health and the reduction of stress, because joyful activities help keep us rooted in the present. 'We have a tendency to think that self-care should involve a trip to a spa and an expensive massage – but allowing yourself to enjoy life is the ultimate in self-care.'

Go on a joy diet

Fetell Lee believes many of us are suffering from 'sensory starvation'. 'We have an array of senses that allow us to interact with the world, yet most of us spend our days in front of a computer. We have hypersensitive fingers and all we give them to do is tap away on a keyboard; we have hypersensitive noses, yet all we give them to smell is recycled air...' She suggests that a fast route to experiencing more joy is indulging in things to make our senses come alive.

When we stop cutting ourselves off from the sensory world, we are less likely to direct that hunger towards things such as food, drink or drugs. The antidote is to put yourself on a joy diet. Start by listing the five senses and, under each, write down tangible things that bring you pleasure. If you struggle with a particular category, that's a clue about where you should focus your attention. This could include anything from cheese on toast, scented bubble bath, a cashmere yoga blanket, Barber's *Adagio for Strings* or a row of pastel painted houses.

In fact, the simple act of writing down the specific things that bring you joy can have immediate effect on your mood! The truth is that it's easy to forget what brings us joy in the first place. You just need to the occasional reminder to bring it back into your life.

GRIEF IS THE PRICE WE PAY FOR LOVE

There is no easy way to deal with loss, be it a bereavement, the end of a relationship or the loss of a job. But heartbreak doesn't have to break you, and there are even positive lessons to be learned.

No one is immune from life's losses and they are an unavoidable part of the human experience but, despite knowing that intellectually, nothing can prepare you for the seismic loss of a loved one. 'The task psychologically is to both face the death, and find a way of living with it,' says Julia Samuel, a therapist specializing in grief. 'Your loss may be of a more complex nature – someone you did not like but for whom you have strong feelings. You need to find a way of accommodating loss while still engaging with life, so grief doesn't overwhelm you. Part of that is to remember that the person may be gone but love never dies.'

Samuel cites another type of grief, which she calls 'living losses'. 'These include divorce or losing your job. Loss also features in events that are usually seen as positive, such as committing to a new relationship, having a child or your offspring getting married. All of those changes require an internal process of your old self adapting to a new version of you. You may have been an independent, single woman who is now tied to a husband and baby. If you find that transition difficult, you might think there is something wrong with you, but it's normal to grieve a past self. If you don't grieve properly, you limit your capacity to engage in your new phase of life and will have less pleasure and joy.'

GRIEF MAPS

One of the most famous models of grief was created by psychiatrist Elisabeth Kubler-Ross. The five stages are denial, anger, bargaining, depression and acceptance. However, Samuel points out that it's not helpful to view these as states that you work through in order. 'Grief is messier and more complex. You can experience all five stages at once or feel each one at different times of day.' A more useful template is that of Margaret Stroebe and Henk Schut – the dual process model of coping with bereavement. 'This is the idea that you are constantly moving between loss and restoration. You might be in pain but distract yourself by doing something enjoyable, then go back to feeling the pain,' explains Samuel. 'This process is as valid for living losses as it is for bereavement. If we go back to the new-mother analogy, you might be feeling awful because you've been awake since 5 am. Then you go to the park and have a lovely time, feel proud of your baby and later get someone to watch them so you can sleep. Over time, you adjust because people are wired to do that. It's only our heads trying to control us that get in the way.'

LIVE YOUR LIFE

Psychologist Gemma Bullivant specializes in grief and transition. 'I believe there are positive aspects that can be pulled from all adversity. I'm not suggesting people try to feel glad after loss, just to notice that there could be beneficial consequences, things you could use to grow.' Bullivant subscribes to researcher Lois Tonkin's 'fried egg' model of grief, in which the yolk represents your grief and the white the rest of your life. 'There's a misconception that, over time, grief grows smaller,' says Bullivant, 'but Tonkin suggests that the rest of your life grows bigger around the grief, so the grief feels smaller.'

THE MATURATION OF MOURNING

Psychotherapist Juliet Rosenfeld, who lost her husband Andrew to cancer a few months after they were married, makes the distinction between grief and mourning, inspired by Sigmund Freud's seminal essay *Mourning and Melancholia*. He defined grief as the savage trauma that occurs at the moment of death, and the evolution of that into mourning. 'Grief is like a volcanic explosion; catastrophic,' says Rosenfeld, 'but life goes on around you. I was doing the food shopping and school run after a couple of days, and soon went back to work. Psychologically, however, I was cut off for

A quarter of all visits to GPs are thought to stem from mental health issues connected to some form of loss. But loss wasn't only classed as bereavement – types of loss include separation from loved ones, incapacitation, migration, relocation, loss of a job, birth of a child and retirement, or professional loss.

a long time. That is grief. I used to think about Andrew hundreds of times a day, but I was functioning.' Rosenfeld believes mourning happens once a person has been allowed to grieve fully. 'Grief is lonely, even if you are surrounded by loving people. I felt isolated and that is a major component of grief. The turning point was when I saw a new therapist three years later, and he said: "I think you're still deeply grieving your husband." That changed things for me and, from that point, I started to recover Andrew, and mourning began. I could bring to mind memories of him and a sense of him being with me, whereas before, I had not felt anything other than: he's dead,' she explains. 'And I think mourning goes on for the rest of a person's life. It's not the depth of the pain that diminishes, it's the regularity. I don't think of him constantly now but, when I do, it's just as painful.'

HOW TO HELP YOURSELF

When we experience loss, we grapple with a tsunami of unpredictable, strong emotions that can be difficult to handle. 'It's helpful to understand that strong emotions, such as heartbreak, are normal, and physiological too,' says Samuel. 'If you measure the brainwaves of someone who puts their hand in ice for 10 minutes with those of someone who is heartbroken, the level of pain and distress is the same. But feelings don't kill you. If you can find a way of letting them run through your system and support yourself through it, you become more resilient, bending with the waves of life, rather than breaking.'

Making a conscious effort to keep your connection alive is important. 'The person has died but the love has not. Find ways to remember them, maybe by looking at photos or cooking their favourite meal.' Samuel believes rituals are healing. 'Light a candle or say a poem or a prayer to commemorate the person. A pilgrimage can also help; a walk you used to do together. Rituals externalize grief, which is otherwise invisible.' Bullivant

uses a grief dimensions grid with clients. 'It is based on the four dimensions of wellbeing: physical, social, emotional and societal. We use the model to assess what's going on in a person's life after loss. How is grief manifesting in those four quadrants of life? You can use the same quadrants to project into the future and ask: How do I want those quadrants to look? What are the areas I want to focus on to make the most of my new reality? What have I discovered about myself during this process? What do I want to reclaim in myself and my life; things I had before my loss? It's not about throwing everything out the window. It's about asking how are you going to define yourself and your approach to life in the future,' she says.

AM I GOING TO BE OK?

Sometimes, the wisest thing you can do is seek professional help. 'Therapy gives you structure. There's a box of time every week just for you to talk about who or what you have lost. In a way, it frees you to get on with your life for the rest of the time,' says Samuel. How do you know when you need help? Samuel says it takes anything between six weeks and three months to get over the initial shock. During this time, it's normal to feel a gamut of emotions. 'After that, there are questions you could ask yourself: Are you feeling resilient and robust? Can you cope with your feelings? Do you have a history of loss, because new losses always bring back previous losses? What support do you have?' She points out that if someone's death was sudden or traumatic, you should expect 'all the normal aspects of grief, but with the volume turned up'. It's useful to consider your relationship with the person. 'Was it a loving relationship without regrets, or was it a complicated one with intense emotional investment? For example, realizing that you're never going to have the parent that you always wanted.' The other red flag telling you that you need help is if you feel that you are not coping, and there's no time limit for that. 'I see people within weeks or months, and others who don't feel ready until years have passed. I had a client who felt fine so went back to work. Then he realized he wasn't sleeping, was fighting with people, couldn't concentrate and felt frightened. Grief feels like fear.'

ANAESTHETIC DELAY

After loss, people may submerge themselves in drugs, alcohol or sex to numb the pain. 'That doesn't mean you can't have a drink now and again,' says Samuel, 'but, if you do one or all of those things all the time in a manic way, it is a warning signal. If it feels as if grief is controlling your behaviour, it is time to seek help.' Samuel is cautious about using medication such as antidepressants to get through grief. 'Grief is a natural process that we need to allow to run its course while we adapt.' But she adds: 'There are people who have other personality and emotional difficulties that are triggered by loss. They may need medication to bring stability and avoid suicidal feelings, for example.'

I'VE GOT YOU

Supporting someone through loss is challenging. 'The best analogy I can think of is: when a child falls over and grazes their knee, they're in agony. There's nothing you can do about the pain, but you can hug them through it,' says Rosenfeld. 'The pain of loss is similar. People who didn't necessarily say much held me emotionally. They let me talk about Andrew – not only about his death, but about him as a person.' Acknowledging the immensity of the loss is crucial. 'In their desire to make you feel better, people try to diminish it,' says Samuel. 'It's better not to say "she had a good innings" or "at least she had a peaceful death". Avoid platitudes that do not match what the person is feeling, which is that they don't want their loved one to be dead. 'All you have to say is "I'm sorry X has died", then follow their lead. If they want to talk, listen. If they don't want to talk, don't force them. Don't do that tilted head "tell me..." expression. And be there for the long haul. Show up, go for walks and watch films together. Don't give it three months and then you're done. Keep bringing the proverbial lasagne and let them set the agenda.'

THE EMOTIONS OF GRIEF

YOUR FEELINGS while grieving are complex and wide-ranging:

- Shocked or numb.
- Sad.
- Anxious or agitated.
- Exhausted.
- Relieved.
- Guilty.
- Angry.
- Calm.
- Lacking in purpose.
- Resentful.

LET IT GO

Learn the healing art of forgiveness for health
and happiness.

Many of us harbour grudges – it's a perfectly natural defence mechanism
– but these self-destructive feelings have a huge impact on our physical
and emotional health.

'Most of us struggle with forgiveness,' says transpersonal
psychotherapist Hilda Burke (hildaburke.co.uk). 'We rack up the wrongs
done to us and hold them deep in our hearts. The irony is that by denying
forgiveness, we do wrong against ourselves, the very ones we are trying
to protect.'

'Put very simply: negative emotions are damaging for our health,'
says Francesca Moresi, psychologist and psychotherapist at the Ambrose
Clinic in Knightsbridge (susieambroseclinic.com). 'The benefits of
forgiveness are essential for our emotional and physical wellbeing,' she
says, adding that forgiveness allows people to let noxious feelings go and
to rediscover positive emotions such as compassion and tenderness.

Dr Frederic Luskin, director of the Stanford University Forgiveness
Project runs global workshops on forgiveness therapy, including those
for people who suffered from the violence in Northern Ireland and
the attacks on the World Trade Center on 9/11. He says: 'The practice
of forgiveness has been shown to reduce anger, hurt depression and
stress and leads to greater feelings of hope, peace, compassion and self-
confidence. Practising forgiveness leads to healthy relationships as well
as physical health. It also influences our attitude which opens the heart to
kindness, beauty, and love.'

Learning to forgive can help to boost our physical health too, and
it has been linked to improved heart health, a strong immune system
and decreased stress levels. A study in the *Journal of Behavioral Medicine*
found people who were forgiving had lower blood pressure than people
who weren't. Research from the University of Wisconsin-Madison

SAY WHAT?

SOME INSPIRATIONAL FORGIVENESS QUOTES WE LOVE

Forgiveness is the attribute of the strong.
Mahatma Gandhi

Forgiveness gives you back the laughter and the lightness in your life.
Joan Lunden

He who is devoid of the power to forgive is devoid of the power of love.
Martin Luther King, Jr.

It is one of the greatest gifts you can give, to forgive yourself. Forgive everybody.
Maya Angelou

Always forgive your enemies, nothing annoys them so much.
Oscar Wilde

showed that people holding a grudge had more heart problems than those who let go of resentments. Even just *thinking* about forgiving someone can help. When 71 subjects in a study were told to think about letting go of a grudge, their cardiovascular and nervous system functioning improved.

So the benefits of forgiveness are pretty obvious, but how do we go about achieving this elusive state of grace, to accept that a negative circumstance has occurred and then let go of those negative feelings?

'The key to happiness and inner peace is, without question, the ability to express hurt followed by the ability to express forgiveness, followed by the ability to be grateful,' says celebrity therapist Maris Peer (marisapeer. com). 'These three things are all important. When we express our hurt we feel heard and we have closure; once we have expressed hurt we are able to forgive and move on,' she says, adding: 'Remember that we forgive others not for their sakes but for ours.'

Some experts work on the premise that forgiveness lives more in the heart than the head. 'That means forgiveness is something we have to feel rather than think,' says Nick Seneca Jankel, psychological coach. 'Many people start off knowing that forgiveness is rationally the right thing to do, but their emotional pain prevents them from being able to do it.' Jankel, the author of the self-help manual *Switch On*, focuses on emotional techniques such as developing empathy for the other person, and compassion for others and ourselves as well. 'It is very hard to show compassion towards other people until we have first forgiven ourselves for our own foibles,' he points out.

NINE STEPS TO FORGIVENESS

THESE ARE THE EMPOWERING self-help techniques outlined in the 'Forgive For Good' workshops:

1. Know exactly how you feel about what happened and be able to articulate what about the situation is not OK. Then, tell a trusted couple of people about your experience.

2. Make a commitment to yourself to do what you have to do to feel better. Forgiveness is for you and not for anyone else.

3. Forgiveness does not necessarily mean reconciliation with the person that hurt you, or condoning their action. What you are after is to find peace. Forgiveness can be defined as the 'peace and understanding that come from blaming that which has hurt you less, taking the life experience less personally, and changing your grievance story'.

4. Get the right perspective on what is happening. Recognize that your primary distress is coming from the hurt feelings, thoughts and physical upset you are suffering now, not what offended you or hurt you two minutes – or ten years – ago. Forgiveness helps to heal those hurt feelings.

5. At the moment you feel upset, practise a simple stress management technique to soothe your body's fight-or-flight response.

6. Give up expecting things from other people, or your life, that they do not choose to give you. Recognize the 'unenforceable rules' you have for your health or how you or other people must behave. Remind yourself that you can hope for health, love, peace and prosperity, and work hard to get them.

7. Put your energy into looking for another way to get your positive goals met rather than through the experience that has hurt you. Instead of mentally replaying your hurt, seek out new ways to get what you want.

8. Remember that a life well lived is your best revenge. Instead of focusing on your wounded feelings and thereby giving the person who caused you pain power over you, learn to look for the love, beauty and kindness around you. Forgiveness is about personal power.

9. Amend your grievance story to remind you of the heroic choice to forgive.

What is important is to remember that learning to let go of negative feelings and behavioural patterns is an ongoing process. 'Forgiveness is an aware, proactive choice, it does not just happen and it requires time,' says Francesca Moresi. 'You don't come to a place of forgiveness and that's it. Reminders emerge that bring the hurtful incidents back to us. When that happens, we have to do the forgiveness work again and again.'

Luskin, author of *Forgive For Good: A Proven Prescription for Health and Happiness*, agrees. 'You can't just will forgiveness. What I teach is that you can create conditions where forgiveness is more likely to occur. There are specific practices that diminish hostility and self-pity, and increase positive emotions, so it becomes more likely that a genuine, heartfelt release of resentment will occur. We suggest to people that since we have to move on anyway, we might as well do so with an open heart. The closer we can come to loving, accepting and being peaceful, the better chance we have of a good life. It's just that simple.'

TRY THIS!

SOME SIMPLE SELF-HELP THERAPIES FOR FORGIVENESS

Hawaiian wisdom

This is a simple yet extremely powerful forgiveness practice to try, based on the ancient Hawaiian wisdom tradition of Ho'oponopono, according to Nick Seneca Jankel. When you feel stressed out by something that is hard to let go of, repeat the words 'Thank you. I love you. I am sorry. Please forgive me,' over and over, feeling their meaning within. The words don't have to be focused on anyone; just on the universe itself. They can even be words you say to yourself. The key thing is to *feel* them in your emotions, not just think or say them. Notice your stress levels drop as you repeat and emotionalize the words. Notice your heart feel more expansive and your muscles relaxing all over.

Practise loving kindness

One of the most powerful ways to find forgiveness is the Buddhist loving kindness meditation, also known as metta bhavana. This practice involves cultivating and sending out a sense of love and wellbeing to everyone:

- First, bring your attention to your heart region, take a few breaths, form an image of yourself in the sitting position, and recall that all beings wish to be happy and free from suffering.
- Think of another living being who naturally makes you smile. This could be a child, your grandmother, your cat or dog—whomever naturally brings happiness to your heart. Then say: 'May you be safe. May you be happy. May you be healthy. May you live with ease.'
- Repeat softly and gently, feeling the importance of your words.

This can then be expanded and directed to yourself, to someone you feel neutral about, to someone you find difficult, to your entire community and the rest of the world. Try it – it's very effective!

Learn gratitude

Actively being grateful is one of the most powerful tools for healing and spiritual growth, according to Francesca Moresi. Every morning, before your day starts, name five things you are grateful for in your life. This can be anything, even the smallest and simple things. Grateful people are happier. Those who forgive are the happiest of all.

Try petal power

'Making peace with our past is important as unresolved resentments and being unable to forgive prevent us from being happy in the present,' says Bach Flower Remedy practitioner Alexandra Bacon of Lotus Therapeutics. If you're feeling sorry for yourself or resentful of others, try the remedy willow. If you find yourself with a touch of the green-eyed monster and have feelings of envy and spite, try holly. Or if you find yourself holding onto the past, try honeysuckle. For more info, visit bachremedies.com.

HOW TO HAVE HEALTHY RELATIONSHIPS

Our state of mind plays a massive part in the way we interact with other people, from friends and family to work colleagues and lovers. Learning how to balance our emotions is one of the building blocks of happy and healthy relationships with others. Here's how...

WHAT IS YOUR ATTACHMENT STYLE?

Are you your own worst enemy when it comes to relationships? If you can understand why you respond to others the way you do – in love, friendships and at work – you can learn to build better connections.

Have you ever felt baffled at your ability to sabotage a relationship just as it gets off the ground? Or do you consistently choose partners who aren't ready to commit? Chances are your attachment style is in operation. Attachment is like default programming that runs silently in the background, invisibly influencing your behaviour and choices. It can override your logical mind, which is why you can find yourself stuck in a relationship that you know is bad for you, or constantly anxious about how well you're doing at work, despite a positive appraisal. Scientists have identified four main attachment styles: secure, anxious, avoidant and chaotic (also known as disorganized). Thanks to attachment research, we know that the quality and consistency of the attention and love we get from birth has a lasting impact on the way our brain and nervous system develop. Researchers such as psychologist Phillip Shaver have shown that our childhood attachment styles have a major influence over our adult relationships, and conflict in our lives and communication problems with others can be attributed to clashing attachment styles. According to studies, our attachment style can also have an impact on our resilience to stress.

The comforting news is that attachment styles can evolve – 30 per cent of us change our attachment styles as adults. Good relationships can help us reset our attachment style and, as we grow in emotional intelligence and self-awareness, we can spot unhelpful patterns and consciously choose different responses. Take our test (overleaf) to reveal your attachment style, and find out how you can work with it to have better relationships.

How do you bond? Attachment style is a window into your psyche and, when you see through it clearly, the way you connect can evolve and your relationships can thrive.

1 In your friendship group, you're the:
- ♥ Steady one who can be relied on
- ◆ One who's most sensitive and easily upset
- O Maverick who does their own thing
- ■ One with the most problems

2 How much time do you spend worrying about what people think of you?
- ■ It varies – sometimes you couldn't care less, sometimes it's an obsession
- ♥ Very little – you instinctively know with whom you connect
- ◆ Far too much – it's a constant background worry
- O Not a lot – what you think about other people is more important to you

3 When a new person joins your social circle or workplace, you tend to:
- ♥ Take a relaxed approach to getting to know them
- O Keep your distance until you've sussed them out
- ◆ Feel anxious about making a good impression
- ■ Go with your gut reaction about whether you like or dislike them

4 If you fall out with a friend, your instinct is to:
- ■ Let everyone know you are the victim
- O Avoid contact until things blow over
- ◆ Do whatever you can to make things right
- ♥ Ask to talk so you can both understand what's happened

5 Time alone for you is:
- ♥ A chance to do some life admin or just relax

- ◆ Your least favourite way of spending time
- O Often when you feel the most comfortable
- ■ A trigger for self-destructive behaviour like a binge

6 When you're not in a romantic relationship, you feel:
- ■ Convinced you'll be alone forever
- ♥ Happy on your own but open to meeting someone new
- ◆ In limbo, like life's on hold
- O That life is a lot simpler in many ways

7 When you bring to mind your closest relationships, the underlying emotion is:
- ♥ Gratitude and happiness
- ◆ Happiness mixed with anxiety
- O A low-level sense of unease
- ■ A mix of excitement, fear and anger

8 When your mood takes a downturn, you tend to:
- O Crave time alone so you can work out what's going on
- ■ Comfort-eat or binge-drink to take the edge off
- ♥ Make more time for self-care and bonding with good friends
- ◆ Vent to anyone who will listen to you about how you're feeling

9 For you, a relationship tends to end when:
- ♥ It's obvious that it's just not going to work out
- ◆ You can't seem to get what you need from the other person
- O You begin to feel trapped or uninterested
- ■ It starts to make you feel unwell or destabilized

10 When you are feeling upset, people know because you:
- ◆ Ask for more reassurance than usual
- O Get quiet or withdraw socially
- ■ Go off the rails a bit
- ♥ Let people know by explaining how you feel

Circle the answers that most apply to you, then add them up at the end. Read the section relating to the symbol you circled most (on the next few pages) to reveal your attachment style and how it affects your relationships, then find out how to flourish within your style.

IF YOU CIRCLED MAINLY ◆
YOUR ATTACHMENT TYPE: ANXIOUS

Anxious types are tuned into others' emotions and are hyper-vigilant for signs of disapproval. MRI studies on the brains of anxious types have shown that the areas related to loss are easily activated and those for calming down emotions are under-activated, which is why you can feel as if your emotions hijack you.

There may also be a genetic connection – anxious types have a specific pattern of dopamine receptor DRD2 allele. How it influences attachment is still unclear, but we know genes influence areas of the brain linked with feelings of both bonding and reward.

Anxious types may have experienced inconsistent messages from caregivers growing up, so feel as if love and acceptance can be taken away at any moment. Good parents can create anxious children if they are dealing with severe stress, grief, trauma, depression or isolation, which may deplete their capacity to give consistent attention. Children of divorce can develop an anxious attachment style if they feel responsible for driving away one of their parents. Secure types can become anxious if they suffer emotional abuse that undermines their self-belief. Your loved one gets a lot of your attention because being close to people makes you feel good, but fear and anxiety are triggered when you feel your loved one pull away, and you can sabotage relationships with your insecurity, constant need for reassurance and jealousy.

Strengths:

You need close relationships to feel safe, so you put in a lot of effort. You probably have a core group of close friends and you make them feel needed and valued. In romance, you have the capacity for great intimacy and closeness, and can create a special relationship with the right person.

ANXIOUS TYPES AT WORK

YOU CAN BECOME a people pleaser and find it hard to say no in an effort to gain approval – but resentment can build if you feel you're being exploited. You may see criticism where none was intended and be fearful of doing the wrong thing, which can lead to a compulsion to recheck emails and go over your work. You may minimize or overlook positive feedback and magnify things that go wrong. Anxious types can be prone to impostor syndrome, which manifests as procrastination or perfectionism.

Weaknesses:

You can drive people away with your insecurity. Relationships consume a lot of your energy, sometimes to the detriment of other areas of your life. Your imagination can go into overdrive, obsessing about whether your partner wants to be with you. You may personalize others' behaviour as being deliberately hurtful, and can find it hard to move on from relationships that are not right for you.

HOW TO FLOURISH AS AN ANXIOUS TYPE

1. Connect with your values

Rather than ruminating on what others may think of you, identify your values and what gives life meaning for you. Instead of looking to others for validation that you are a good person, ask: How closely is my behaviour aligned with my values? How can I bring it closer?

2. Be kind to yourself

Talk to yourself with compassion if you feel insecure – anxious types have a vocal inner critic.

3. Savour time alone

Plan to do something special on a free day.

4. Create a secure base

You do best in long-term relationships where you can grow in confidence. Anxious women often repeat patterns by subconsciously seeking avoidant men who can't meet their needs. Your ideal partner will give you the attention you need without fuelling your insecurities.

5. Stop overthinking

Be aware of the power of your imagination to conjure up scenarios of what others might be thinking or doing. If you feel anxious, distract yourself by going for a walk or calling a friend.

IF YOU CIRCLED MAINLY ♥
YOUR ATTACHMENT TYPE: SECURE

You may be one of the 50 per cent of the population who grew up knowing that you were loved and valued by those you spent most time with. As a baby and child, your caregivers were responsive to your needs. Your feelings were validated and your parents helped you find healthy ways to manage your emotions. Sometimes a secure attachment style develops in adulthood, thanks to positive experiences in relationships or self-awareness and emotional intelligence. Not every secure type is a self-confident extrovert – secure types may struggle with self-doubt and they can be vulnerable to stress and general anxiety, but experiencing adversity does not usually result in you questioning whether you are lovable, or whether you really want to be in a relationship. Secures' default programming includes a belief that love is available for them. Studies show that secure types have high levels of satisfaction, commitment and trust in their relationships.

In romantic relationships, you have a clear sense of what you want and take responsibility for the part you may play when conflict arises. Relationships give your life meaning and you give them the time and attention they need, but you don't get sucked into overthinking them, which frees up energy and headspace to allow other areas of your life to flourish. A relationship with a secure type can create a 'dependence paradox' – the secure base they create allows both partners to become independent person types and develop as individuals.

However, if a secure type ends up in a relationship where they are stonewalled or controlled, they can acquire an anxious or avoidant attachment style out of self-protection.

Strengths:

Secure types tend to be good at communicating and can become unofficial 'communication coaches' at work, helping others resolve conflict and open up. You can create a strong and secure relationship with the right person that also allows both of you freedom to develop as individuals. You 'fight clean' in relationships when conflict arises and are able to focus on what's happened and what needs to change, rather than making personal attacks or going on the defensive. Your emotional system doesn't get too riled up in the face of threat (as with anxious types), but doesn't shut down either (as with avoidant types).

Weaknesses:

Secure types can become rescuers and part with a lot of energy if they get close to an anxious, avoidant or chaotic type. You tend to bring out the best in people but your secure base can be compromised, leaving you questioning your judgement and self-worth if you find yourself in an emotionally unhealthy relationship. Research shows that people with a secure attachment style are more likely than others to forgive their partner for wrongdoing. Secures can, however, become insecure in an ongoing emotionally undermining relationship.

HOW TO FLOURISH AS A SECURE TYPE
1. Watch out for rescuing

Be aware that secure types tend to attract those with chaotic, anxious and avoidant styles. A relationship with a secure type can help other styles become more secure, but it can come at a cost to you. Secure types can become responsible for their partner's wellbeing and may feel convinced that they can make challenging relationships or jobs work. But just because you can get along with everyone doesn't mean you have to – some situations are toxic and you're better off out of them.

2. Don't neglect self-care

Secure types aren't saints – feeling overwhelmed or stressed can have an impact on your mood and you can experience confidence crises at work. Secure types are usually good at looking after themselves, but if self-care falls down your list of priorities, you will be affected.

3. Spend time with other secures

If you do a lot of supporting of other people, make sure you spend time with those who give back and uplift you too.

IF YOU CIRCLED MAINLY 0
YOUR ATTACHMENT PROFILE: AVOIDANT

Sometimes parents who are overwhelmed with stress or dealing with grief or trauma can inadvently give their children the message that their needs are an additional burden with which they cannot cope. Closing off and keeping your emotions to yourself is a smart survival strategy if you grow up believing that you'll be easier to love and accept if you demand as little as possible. Avoidant types often grow up deciding it's best not to rely on others. Sometimes even well-meaning parents can create an avoidant child if they don't know how to cope with strong emotions. Every time you're told not to be 'silly' when you're upset, you're being told that your feelings are bad or that they don't matter. As adults, avoidants have a need for distance and separateness, and assume their drive to get away from a relationship means they're not with the right person. However, they can often feel conflicted – claustrophobic if people get too close, but hurt if they're left out of the inner circle at work and in friendships or if romantic partners seem too distant. Secure personalities can help avoidants open up – but relationships between avoidants and anxious types can be somewhat challenging – an avoidant person can push an anxious type away when they're being needy and sabotage the relationship with hurtful behaviour in order to get the space that they feel they need.

Strengths:

You're self-reliant and self-contained, which leaves you with the capacity to support others through challenging times. You often develop close relationships by being a good listener and you're comfortable with vulnerability as long

AVOIDANT TYPES AT WORK

YOU'RE A SELF-STARTER who can take a maverick approach, rather than being a team player. Avoidants often work long hours, as this structured, boundaried world is a safe way to be with people. You thrive in creative or entrepreneurial environments and may find corporate life claustrophobic, especially any office politics. There may be conflict between your need to fit in and your drive to keep people at arm's length.

Avoidants can be stoic in tough situations and tend to keep their head down and get on with things rather than complain. This wins brownie points but puts you at risk of being used or overlooked when it comes to a promotion or pay rise.

as it's not your own. When relationships get more complicated, you often find it easy to move on as you haven't really opened up.

Weaknesses:

You tend to see differences before you see connections with new people, so can miss out on potential friendships by dismissing people before you get to know them properly. Your self-sufficiency can make people feel as if you don't need them in your life. You can become a 'bottler and exploder', squashing down your resentment until it eventually erupts, much to the bewilderment of the other people involved.

HOW TO FLOURISH AS AN AVOIDANT TYPE

1. Use mindfulness to get in touch with your emotions

Many avoidants are so adept at denying their feelings that it can take time to get back in touch with what they need.

2. Take baby steps towards opening up and sharing what's really going on for you

Even if avoidant types are good at supporting others, they can remain a closed book about their feelings. Start by banning the word 'fine' when people ask you how you are.

3. Find your tribe

Friendships can take time to develop and one-to-ones can feel too intense, but joining a group that has a focus can take the pressure off, allowing relationships to build at a comfortable pace for you.

4. Be upfront about your need for space

Help those closest to you understand that having time away from them helps keep the relationship happy and ongoing for you.

5. Keep a gratitude journal

Jot down the benefits of having relationships with the key people in your life to counterbalance your brain's natural critical tendencies.

IF YOU CIRCLED MAINLY ■
YOUR ATTACHMENT PROFILE: CHAOTIC

You could be one of the 5 per cent of people with a chaotic attachment style, also known as 'disorganized'. Chaotic attachment is caused when the caregiver that you relied upon as a child was also a source of fear, which can lead to a sense of fragmentation, causing you to shut down from painful feelings. People with a chaotic attachment style often grew up with a parent who was abusive or struggling with addiction. Chaotic types live on an emotional rollercoaster and can be hijacked by their feelings, which railroads their life and relationships. Chaotics have a talent for self-sabotage, which may manifest in an eating disorder or self-harm, or just a compulsion to cause disruption when things are going well for them. Not surprisingly, you crave a release from your feelings, but your self-soothing can turn into self-medication and become a problem in itself. You need intimacy, but have a deep mistrust that anyone really has your best interests at heart. You can also feel powerless in relationships and resort to playing games or making your partner jealous to gain a sense of control.

When we grow up lacking a core belief that we are entitled to respect or to get our needs met, we have to resort to more manipulative ways – so, if you've been looking forward to spending some time with your partner on Saturday, then find out they've arranged to go out for the day, instead of telling them that you feel disappointed, you launch an attack, accusing them of being selfish and never being there for you.

Strengths:
Chaotics can develop resilience and, if they have the right mindset and self-awareness, will learn a lot about human relationships from their experiences. The challenge is to counteract your natural cynical tendency and assumption that no one has your best interests at heart. Given the right circumstances, chaotics can flourish in their relationships.

Weaknesses:

People with a chaotic attachment style can get addicted to the highs and lows of relationships, and can equate drama and conflict with spark and connection. When they meet a secure type, they may be tricked into thinking there is no spark between them because the relationship isn't an adrenaline-fuelled rollercoaster ride.

HOW TO FLOURISH AS CHAOTIC TYPE

1. Self-awareness is key

Consider professional support to help you understand your triggers and learn healthy ways to get your needs met. Learning the difference between assertive and aggressive is crucial, and how to get your point across without either attacking other people or becoming defensive with them.

2. Seek out stable secure types to bring out the best in you

Chaotic types need a secure base – a key relationship with someone who is emotionally there for you and provides you with support, but also empowers you to find your own way and learn from your mistakes. A positive relationship with a secure partner, friend, counsellor, teacher or colleague can result in you developing an 'earned secure attachment'.

3. Be kind to yourself

Chaotics often lack confidence, and studies show that self-compassion is an effective way of building it.

4. Rewrite your narrative

Keep a journal to explore a new perspective on your life story and see where you have autonomy and strength to influence your experience of life. Making sense of your past can help free you from it.

5. Soothe your nervous system

Chaotic types spend a lot of time in hyper-regulated fight-or-flight mode, which makes it hard to access rational thinking. You will flourish if you spend time doing something that teaches you how to self-regulate.

TRUTH BE TOLD

Has people pleasing and not saying how you feel and what you need led you into awkward situations? Learn how to be honest and authentic when communicating in your relationships, so you can find your voice and express your emotions and opinions effectively.

If you're an inveterate people pleaser, you might baulk at the idea of being even partially honest. What's wrong with keeping everyone happy? Quite a lot, as it happens. 'Without honest communication, you get boredom and stagnation,' says couple and relationship psychotherapist Matt Davies. 'People pleasing leads to boring relationships. It also leads to boring sex between partners, because when you're not being honest, when you're aiming to make the other party happy, you're placating.

There's this sense of merging.' Davies says therapists often refer to these types of partnerships as 'babes in the wood' couples. 'Everything between them is always just beautiful, but there's no spark, no fire! In therapy, we often focus on the need for partners to differentiate. Achieving that requires each of you to be vulnerable, which in turn builds greater intimacy and excitement. If you're willing to show yourself as you really are, that actually helps the other partner feel safer. Chances are good that they will also harbour some fear about not being good enough. So, when you reveal your vulnerability to them, they're thinking, 'Oh, they're just like me, so I have nothing to fear,'' says Davies.

SPEAK UP GENTLY WITHOUT FALLING OUT

If you've never been in the habit of speaking up for yourself, doing so can feel daunting. But there's no need to blurt out everything that's on your mind in one conversation. Sam Owen, relationship coach and author of *Happy Relationships: 7 Simple Rules to Create Harmony and Growth* suggests starting out mildly. Say, for example, that your partner or friend has strong views about where to go for dinner and you always go along with them. 'Try saying something like, "Actually, I'd quite like to try a new place I read about." Or, if you want to go further, you might say: "I've been thinking... I've not really spoken up much in the past about where I'd like to go for dinner." So, you're kind of explaining yourself in a way that makes it feel softer and easier to broach.'

Owen also points out that if you want someone to see your point of view or change their behaviour, it's always more effective if you explain why. 'If you do that, you're giving them credit for understanding but, more importantly, you're more likely to get them on board with it if they understand the reasoning behind it.'

PUT THE PAST BEHIND YOU

The golden rule, according to Owen, is to focus a difficult conversation on your goals and desires, rather than your fears and dislikes. So, for example, if you're tackling your partner about why they never do their share of the chores, resist the temptation to present them with a well-rehearsed list of all the things you do that they never help out with. 'Instead, focus on what you'd like their help with. Try and use positive rather than negative words because research shows that negative, critical words can put both the listener and the speaker into a stress response. When that happens, the other person is only going to become more and more defensive and combative, or run away,' says Owen.

ASK FOR WHAT YOU WANT

Talking honestly about sex, especially if you're no longer enjoying it, can be a minefield. Davies mentions running a workshop series for couples entitled 'Passionate Partnerships'. 'We presented the question – are you a sexy couple or a couple who has sex? Many couples who took part mentioned that they had drifted into being housemates.' Davies asserts that honest communication about sex is about taking risks. 'You are putting yourself on the line and revealing your true self. That is exciting, both for you and your partner, if it's done in the right way. They can see that you're on the edge, in a good way.' The key is not to criticize. 'You might say: "Hey, how about we try X?", rather than saying: "I find you so boring" or "you always want to do this or that". Shift the focus onto something new. Setting another goal sexually is a really exciting ambition for your relationship.' According to Davies, 'sexy couples' are people who take risks every day with micro-doses of communication. 'Every time you dare to say to your partner, "I prefer X", even about little things, keeps the spark alive because its about acknowledging difference. And then that's incredibly appealing because, you know, that's why you were attracted to one another in the first place!'

STEER FRIENDSHIPS IN THE RIGHT DIRECTION

The quality of our friendships is super-important, but the topic is often not addressed in conversations about intimacy and connection. 'I believe that the same rules apply with friends as with any other relationship, even if it perhaps feels like there's less of a commitment with friends,' says Davies. 'Friendships are still about psychological intimacy, being able to say what you're feeling and thinking.' Often, what can happen in close friendships is that we use one another as a safe space to vent about things that are going wrong in our lives. That can be great but can also get out of hand. 'In those cases, there are ways of steering friendships in a more satisfying direction. 'You might say: "Maybe you need to talk this over with somebody as this is powerful stuff. It's quite overwhelming to listen to and I appreciate that you really need to talk it through."' It's getting underneath their feelings and helping them recognize that they've been so busy offloading, they have forgotten to ask about you. In any relationship, there's a danger that one party gets cast in the role of sympathetic listener. 'The way of managing that is to find your assertiveness and begin to take agency in the relationship. Try and begin new conversations, or you could say: "I'd like to bring up something that I'd value your opinion on because I've been worrying about it."' The key thing is to take responsibility for your part in the relationship and not just play the victim and complain about your friend who's always giving you long monologues.

MAKING HONEST CONNECTIONS

If you struggle to express your true feelings in relationships, take this test to find out what you need to do in order to bond more authentically.

1   In a group, you are often the:
- ♥ Peacemaker
- ◆ Outsider
- o Entertainer
- ■ Helper

2   You respond to conflict by:
- ■ Accepting blame and apologizing
- ♥ Working hard to resolve it
- ◆ Stepping back until it blows over
- o Pretending everything is OK

3   Your deepest connections are with people who:
- o Don't expect you to be perfect
- ■ Let you be yourself
- ♥ Can almost read your mind
- ◆ Accept you as you are

4   At the end of a typical day, you often feel:
- ■ Fragmented
- o Anxious
- ◆ Flat
- ♥ Disappointed

5   You're most likely to be put off a difficult conversation because:
- ♥ You just can't find a way to bring it up
- ◆ It makes you feel out of control

o   You worry that you are overreacting

■   It feels wrong to fall out with anyone

6 You are at your best when you feel you're:

♥   Strong and thriving

♦   Sure of your direction

o   Thinking positively

■   Valued and approved of

7 You are naturally drawn to people who seem:

■   Open and authentic

♥   Comfortable in their own skin

♦   Brave and unconventional

o   Grounded and compassionate

8 Sometimes, you just wish you could be more:

♥   Vulnerable

o   Self-compassionate

♦   Spontaneous

■   Assertive

9 When you ruminate on the past, you're most likely to fret about:

♥   Upsetting people

♦   Missing out

o   Messing up

■   Being used

10 The biggest risk of being honest is:

♦   Disruption

o   Discomfort

■   Rejection

♥   Disapproval

Circle the answers that most closely apply to you, then add up the symbols. Read the section (or sections) you circled most, to find out how you can overcome your emotional communication barriers.

WHAT WILL HELP YOU OPEN UP IN RELATIONSHIPS?

IF YOU SCORED MAINLY 0
Self-acceptance

Knowing how you feel is one thing; knowing that it's OK to feel that way is another thing altogether. Do your feelings come with a mental commentary, telling you that you should feel differently, because you have no reason to feel unhappy or discontented? It's no surprise, then, that you may put a lot of effort into changing the way you feel. But if you dial down the judgement and self-criticism, and instead treat your feelings with curiosity, you are more likely to understand where they came from. Does your disquiet at a friend's new relationship or job suggest you're craving a change in your own life? Or is your irritation at a demanding family member really a reaction to your own lack of assertiveness? When we tell ourselves we shouldn't feel a certain way, we shut down a potential source of information. Living more honestly starts with self-acceptance and treating yourself with compassion. When uncomfortable feelings come up, rather than silencing them, try simply asking yourself, 'OK, my dear, what's going on here?'

IF YOU SCORED MAINLY ■
Self-belief

Worrying about what others think of us can become a powerful barrier, keeping us in our comfort zone and undermining our attempts to connect. When you are super-conscious of saying and doing the right thing, you can end up presenting a different 'you' in every relationship. It's true that empathetic attunement is an important part of creating connections – but are you really connecting with others if you always tell them what you think they want to hear? Compromise and putting others first can seem like much safer territory than prioritizing what you want and risking rejection. But when appeasing everyone is your default mode, it can be hard to be honest and tell people what you really feel. It can also be destructive, limiting potentially great relationships from reaching true depth. Feeling connected starts with getting in touch with who you are and what you believe. Simply pausing to check in and ask, 'How am I reacting to this? What are my thoughts and emotions?' is a good start. Then ask, 'Why I am convinced that people can't cope with knowing how I really feel?'

IF YOU SCORED MAINLY ♥
Trust

When you grow up absorbing the message that showing your emotions upsets others, you quickly learn to self-edit to protect the people you love and depend on. Were you told that being grown up means not expecting others to manage your feelings for you? It's true that the ability to self-manage feelings is a part of emotional intelligence but if, somewhere along the line, you start to believe it's only acceptable to reveal a certain type of emotion, you may attract people who like the fact that you ask little of them, allowing their own needs to take centre stage. Others may be drawn to your strength, but later feel frustrated that you never let down your guard. It can be a leap to share how you are feeling when there's no guarantee it will change anything. You have to do so with no expectation of getting an appropriate response – people may be blissfully unaware of what a big deal it is for you to be so honest – but those who really care about you will love being 'let in', and those connections that really matter will deepen and grow.

IF YOU SCORED MAINLY ◆
Awareness

Connecting honestly with others starts by connecting with yourself. A busy life can also disconnect you from your feelings, keeping you stuck in 'doing' mode or living in your head. When your default mode is 'everything is fine', checking in with your emotions can feel risky, throwing your life choices into question and derailing your mood and motivation in the process. But the need to live authentically is a powerful drive in all of us and, in time, it will become harder to ignore. Retreating to the logic of your thoughts, where you can find solutions, can feel like a much safer place from which to operate, rather than being buffeted by emotions. It's true that feelings can be fleeting and change like the weather, but they can also be a barometer of your emotional wellbeing, alerting you to when something needs to change. Try setting a timer on your phone to check in with how you are feeling throughout the day. Take a few minutes to settle yourself, then simply ask, 'What's the weather pattern inside?' Resist labelling or trying to get rid of what you find – just be curious.

HOW TO FIND HARMONY

Bringing balance into your life is all about taking the right emotional approach, whether it's through taking time out to focus on your own wellbeing, building resilience in the face of adversity or learning to be more assertive. Here's how...

DAYDREAMING

Find out how doing nothing, or 'niksen' as the Dutch call it, can improve your health.

It all began with the Danish concept of 'hygge', the delightfully indulgent idea of getting cozy – think candles, blankets, roaring fires and toasting marshmallows. Then came Sweden's 'lagom', which encouraged us to approach life with an 'everything in moderation' mindset. And now there's another wonderfully relaxing and simple concept emerging from the Netherlands... niksen, which simply means 'the art of doing nothing', and it's here to help you reduce the stresses of everyday life.

There's nothing lazy about the powerful impact niksen can have on your emotional wellbeing.

'The Dutch concept of niksen is definitely something we could all take inspiration from in today's ever-busy, switched-on world,' says Bupa Mental Health Nurse Adviser, Caroline Harper (bupa.co.uk/health). Allowing yourself time to sit with your own thoughts, to truly relax and restore, is crucial for aiding stress relief and improving your mental wellbeing. 'Switching off shouldn't be that difficult; yet even when you're home with no plans, it can feel near impossible,' adds Caroline. 'Niksen encourages you to slow down and indulge in some downtime. Forget busying yourself with huge plans, getting FOMO – fear of missing out – from checking what others are doing online, or dealing with work emails and deadline demands; niksen is all about dedicating focused time to just sitting still with your own thoughts.' And despite its idle meaning, there's nothing lazy about the powerful impact it can have on your mental wellbeing.

LET YOUR MIND WANDER
Taking time to do nothing and let your thoughts flow freely not only helps to reduce stress and anxiety, but is also said to boost productivity and creativity. Studies have found that letting your mind wander can

leave you feeling inspired about achieving your goals and give you the clarity needed for achieving them. So-called 'procrastination' can actually equal productivity in the long run. It differs from mindfulness in that mindfulness encourages you to be present in the moment, whereas niksen asks you to do quite the opposite: to lose yourself in a daydream. 'Allow boredom to occur and stop viewing it negatively,' says Caroline. 'Being busy has somehow become something to be proud of, while sitting around with nothing to do almost feels shameful, yet niksen turns that on its head, taking the idea of simplicity and quality of life to a blissful new level.

Giving your brain some downtime is good for you, providing a counterbalance to the pressure of always needing to 'do' something.

TRY IT YOURSELF!

EXPERTS SUGGEST you should practise niksen as often as you need, but try to make a little time every day. Start off small with just 5 minutes and as it becomes a part of your routine, increase the time you spend on it. Half an hour a day is ideal. Here, Caroline Harper shares her tips for when niksen works best and how to get in the right mindset to do it...

AT WORK

It might seem odd to suggest doing absolutely nothing while at work, but a spot of niksen on your lunch break could be just the ticket. Even when you're doing nothing, your brain is processing information. The idea is that when it's allowed to relax and recharge, solutions, ideas and creative concepts come to you more freely when you get back to it. The key is not to overthink.

LYING IN BED

By its very nature, being in bed suggests you're at the perfect point of doing nothing. This is the ideal time for niksen. So why not put down your book, switch off your phone and let your thoughts run away with you as you lie in bed? It might even help you drift off to sleep.

WHILE CRAFTING

There aren't many activities you can do while practising niksen, but crafting is one of them.

The repetitive motion of knitting, for example, allows you to lose yourself in your own thoughts and let your mind wander. Make sure the task requires minimal effort – if you can do it on autopilot, this allows you the right headspace for daydreaming.

OUT WALKING

Intense exercise requires concentration, not to mention a goal to aim for – so this is not ideal niksen time. However, the one exercise you can lose yourself in is walking. Choose a picturesque route and wander idly with no set route or intended destination. Keep thoughts of work or what's for dinner at bay, ideally!

AROUND THE HOUSE

Ultimately, niksen should be done when you have nothing else to do and with no other distractions at all. The best way to do this is to carve out some time while you're at home. Simply sit back on the sofa and relax. Don't lift a finger. Gaze out of the window into the distance and just be calm. It's this pursuit of nothingness that makes niksen so unique.

HOW TO SUPERCHARGE YOUR MORNING ROUTINE

Feel energized and get your morning off to a great start with these top tips...

Get up a little earlier to make time for a more positive morning routine, and you'll find you have more energy and focus throughout the day. What's more, by giving yourself a little extra time and space at the start of each day, you'll not only be honouring and prioritizing your own self-care, but the mental clarity you'll feel at having quietened your mind and looked after yourself fully will also see you more likely to achieve the goals you've set yourself for the rest of the day. Here are six ways to ensure you get out of bed on the right foot each morning:

1. DRINK A GLASS OF WATER

Keep a glass or bottle of water on your bedside table, so you can sip it as soon as you wake up in the morning. This helps to kickstart hydration, which is good for both your mind and body.

2. MAKE TIME FOR MEDITATION

Starting your morning with a meditation is a great way to embrace the coming day, and it doesn't have to be long – just 5–10 minutes can do wonders for your state of mind. 'Meditation presses the rest button, allowing you to start each day as a blank canvas,' says Steve Chamberlain, life coach. 'It also helps to create separation between you and your thoughts, which can enable you to be more present and focused throughout the day.' While it's tempting to meditate from the comfort of your bed, this

might not be the best idea. 'Choose a place that feels comforting or cosy in your house — you could grab a blanket so you're warm. Initially, simply close your eyes and allow your mind and thoughts to do whatever they want to do, then you can choose to focus on your breath, returning to it each time your mind wanders.'

3. STRETCH

Gently moving your body with a short yoga flow or simple stretch feels fantastic — and it's a good way of being mindful first thing in the morning. 'A morning stretch will start to get your energy flowing and, by consciously focusing your attention on each muscle as you stretch, it allows you to mindfully come into the present moment,' says Chamberlain. 'Practised daily, over time you'll notice you have more flexibility and energy throughout your day.'

4. SET A POSITIVE INTENTION

Your mind is a powerful tool, so programme it to help you make the most of the day ahead. 'Set an intention for who you choose to be and how you will choose to show up in each moment,' suggests Chamberlain. 'Life

rewards intent and action, so you'll likely start to notice more positive results playing out. Keep your intention short and to the point, which will allow you to easily align with it throughout your day – "I choose to be courageous in everything I do" or "I am open and present" are good examples of a positive daily intention.'

5. TAKE A COLD SHOWER

As horrible as it might sound, having a cold (or cool) shower – even for just 30 seconds or a minute – has many health benefits, with studies showing it can help with everything from boosting endorphins (the happy hormone), to improving your circulation and supporting your immune system. 'It might seem unpleasant, but a cold shower shocks you into the present moment and wakes up all of your senses,' says Chamberlain. 'Start with a 10-second cold blast before turning to warm and gradually building up.'

6. EAT A NUTRITIOUS BREAKFAST

Often hailed as the most vital meal of the day, eating a nutritious breakfast has been shown to improve concentration, support digestion and even help to protect your heart. What's more, studies show that your body is better able to process nutrients in the morning, meaning that the first meal of the day can have a significant impact on your overall health. Opt for a healthier, more substantial choice, like porridge topped with fruit, or avocado on seeded toast.

HOW TO FLOURISH

You can use challenges to transform your life in a positive way. Here's how...

Thriving in the face of deep instability is not easy – in fact it always demands a level of discomfort. There is no magic wand that will make our painful experiences vanish. At times, the path may be devastating, and we may feel stuck and fear that happiness will never return. It's important to understand that thriving isn't about making life comfortable and fun, it's about finding purpose and making our own unique contribution.

BORN TO COPE

Evolution demands that we expand to become what we need to become when things fall apart. It is our challenge to find resilience and meaning in the tragedies and fears that confront us. In discovering ways of dealing with these events, we have the possibility of alchemizing our experience and turning the base metal of pain into the gold of wisdom, understanding enrichment and purpose. The following practices will help to build emotional resilience, so that when the inevitable storms blow across our path, we have a tool kit that we are able to seamlessly bring into play.

1. Bear witness

We cannot fix anyone and, even when we love someone and want them to be happy, we still can't make everything OK. The process of change is slow and evolutionary – there isn't a magic solution for every situation, but if we are willing and able to bear witness with authenticity and integrity, then we bring the best we can to every scenario that arises in life.

Exercise:

Next time you find yourself with someone who is unhappy or angry, practise bearing witness to them. Don't judge or try to find solutions. Rather than sympathize, notice what is happening inside you as you

listen. Often, when we feel disturbed, our breathing quickens and, in slowing it down, we give ourselves an extra resource. Let yourself connect with your bodily sensations as you continue relating. Become aware of your breathing and your ability to maintain eye contact. In holding the gaze of another, you are reassuring them that what they are saying isn't overwhelming. In this practice, you will discover a deep capacity and interest in others. As with any practice, there are no quick fixes. You're retraining yourself to be authentic with others and, as you pursue this, you will notice when you are truly bearing witness and when you are pretending. Don't judge yourself, but when you notice your lack of presence, draw your attention back, either by eye contact, breathing or honest communication. Observe your human propensity to switch off and make a conscious choice to bring your attention to what is happening in front of you. Flex this muscle and it will serve you automatically after a while. Expand this practice into everyday life. When you walk past trees, observe their differences and beauty. When you get on the train, refrain from using your phone and going into your own world. Let yourself be someone who drinks in the environment around you.

2. Overcome difficulties with kindness and honesty

Slaying your dragons with compassion is the art of speaking difficult truths that are hard for everyone to hear and painful for you to suppress. To slay your dragons with compassion is to embody these two basic principles:

- Always endeavour to speak what is absolutely true for you.
- Never hurt another person more than is necessary.

Exercise:

The next time you need to say something difficult to another person, don't run away. Commit to the conversation. It's important to find the right place and the right time. Sometimes we may want to make it easier for the other person, so we might choose to have the discussion on their turf, for example. Timing is equally important. It's not beneficial to open a challenging dialogue about something important when you are exhausted. Choose a time when your energy is optimal. Seek wise counsel. Often, when we look for support while we are wounded or vulnerable, we want friends who will make us feel better. However, if we are to look for wisdom in ourselves and others, we don't need 'yes' men. We need compassionate and wise friends. Ask your friends to honestly show you where your blind spots may be. When you start a tough conversation, consciously slow your breathing and make eye contact. Be willing to hear the other person's perspective so you have a fuller picture. Look for a win-win situation and apply the two principles of truth and not hurting the other person more than is necessary.

3. Allow pain to change you and your life

When we suffer, we have a choice to be crushed or transformed. We either mourn and grow, or switch off and curse the world. It is in our best interest to surrender to what is being lived inside us and find meaning and purpose through it.

Exercise:

When you are experiencing pain or loss, choose to let it in. When the feelings arise, spend 10 minutes breathing deeply, focusing on your breaths. When your mind starts to wander, be gentle with yourself and keep bringing your attention back to your breath. Our first instinct around pain is to tighten, distract or run. Instead, observe the impact the pain is having on you and recognize that by slowing down, it is possible to allow the pain to just be. Other ways of dealing with pain are:

- Walk in nature.
- Talk to a trusted friend.
- Seek creative expression in which you honour the event that caused the pain.
- Read stories of those who have engaged with their pain with grace and skill. Psychiatrist Viktor Frankl's *Man's Search for Meaning*, an autobiographical account of how he found spiritual power in the depravity of Nazi concentration camps, is one example. Allow such wisdom to take root in your psyche.
- Listen to music inspired by suffering and let yourself absorb the quality of the lyrics and depth of sound. For me, it's Eric Clapton's *Tears in Heaven* and Nick Cave's album, *Ghosteen* – both written out of the experience of losing a child.

HOW TO ADAPT AND THRIVE IN DIFFICULT TIMES

Acclaimed psychotherapist Julia Samuel gives these words of advice to develop resilience and navigate life's challenges.

Create a good relationship with yourself

'The relationship you have with yourself is the pillar that influences every other relationship in your life. It is central to your wellbeing,' says Samuel. Write a journal, discover what triggers you in terms of negative emotions and how to handle those triggers in the healthiest way possible. Every night, jot down three things for which you are grateful.

Create good relationships with others

Find ways to communicate your love and what you need and learn to have difficult conversations. Find ways to repair a rupture after a row. Listen with your heart, speak honestly and make your key relationships a priority in your life.

Manage your emotions

Be aware of HALT: Hungry, Angry, Lonely, Tired. If you are feeling one of those, you are vulnerable to responding in an inappropriate way. Remember, feelings are not facts. You become more emotionally intelligent when you can identify your emotions, gaining clarity on how to respond to difficult situations.

Keep your focus on today

Practise holding your attention on the present moment – the task at hand. Breathe and plan what you need to do today.

Cultivate a good relationship with the mind/body

What you are thinking and feeling affects your physical self and vice

versa. Make a clear decision to exercise every day, follow a relaxation and meditation practice, eat well and be aware of what you're watching and listening to every day – is it positive?

Learn to be assertive and say no with confidence

Introduce boundaries, which are crucial to our sense of order in a world that can seem overwhelming.

Structure stabilizes – it is a foundation when your world feels shaky

Develop beneficial habits, such as exercise first thing, soothing pastimes and getting enough sleep.

This focusing technique will calm you and enable you to meet the day:

Close your eyes and breathe deeply and slowly, in through your nose, out through your mouth, three times. Move your attention around your body until you find the place with the most sensation. Breathe into that place. Find a word to describe that place... Does it have a shape or colour? Is it hard or soft? Create an image for it. If the image could speak, what would it say? Follow where the image takes you.

THE DEVIL INSIDE

You know that part of you that says 'just do it' when you probably really shouldn't? Fret not, your conflicting selves can co-operate.

When it comes to making wise choices – getting up early to run, resisting the third cocktail, not messaging that ex you want to cut ties with – it often feels as though we're two people living in one body. One of your personalities, Virtuous You, heads to bed confident of leaping up at 6 am, or arrives at the party certain you'll limit yourself to one drink – but the one who's actually faced with the option of diving back under

Rather than battling the devil inside you, try to view yourself in the third person, treating yourself as a friend.

the covers or accepting the next negroni is weak-willed Hedonist You, who can't imagine what Virtuous You was thinking! If your self-disciplined personality could bring the other into line, life might run more smoothly – but that's the problem: when the moment of truth arrives, Virtuous You is nowhere to be seen.

However, all is not lost. With a little ingenuity, your two selves can communicate. The easiest way is for Virtuous You to make environmental changes, making it more difficult for the hedonist to misbehave, like a kindly parent installing a stair gate to stop a toddler from hurting themselves. Remove unhealthy food from your house, for example, and it'll be much harder to binge on junk in the middle of the night; prebook the taxi home for 10.30 pm and it's more likely that you'll actually leave at that time. A harsher tactic is 'strategic precommitment': write a cheque to an organization that you dislike, then make a friend promise to send it if you break your vow.

Another approach focuses less on battling yourself, and more on self-compassion: when tempted to break a promise to yourself, think of yourself as acting for the benefit of the person you'll become in the future. It's a curious truth that we often find it easier to help a friend make good choices than to help ourselves do the same, because we subconsciously believe we don't deserve such kindness. Seeing your actions as a goodwill gesture to your future self gets you over that barrier; you get to indulge your preference for helping other people, except that, this time, the 'someone else' is you.

The broader point here is that you can get useful distance on your problems by adopting a third-person perspective; treating yourself as one of your friends. We tend to think we must have the best vantage point on our personal issues because we're inside our own minds but, in reality, this often means we can't see the wood for the trees. Research shows that journalling about, or talking to, yourself in the third person – even addressing yourself by name – can make the difference: rather than getting caught up in the details, you see your situation in a broad outline and the way forward is clearer. If you can't solve the problem of feeling like two people, at least you can turn it into a net benefit – for both of you.

BE MORE ASSERTIVE

Always at the mercy of others' needs and wants? Here are some tools to develop your firmness with fairness.

- Make a list of the people who treat you with respect and those who take advantage of you.
- Make a note of when and with whom you can assert your boundaries.
- What are the costs and the benefits of your people-pleasing behaviour?
- Answer this question: What do I believe will happen if I say no?

ASSERTIVENESS TECHNIQUES

Assertiveness is about the right to be treated with equal respect. It's about learning what is fair, and balancing your own rights, wants and needs with those of others. Here are some techniques to help you practise assertiveness:

- Trust your gut – being assertive is about developing the habit of noticing your feelings and responses.
- Don't explain or apologize excessively when refusing a request or saying no.
- Consider what it says about the other person if they start bullying you or persuading you to change your mind.
- Buy yourself some time and don't respond immediately with a knee-jerk yes.
- Be aware of your body language. Ensure that you are not smiling or using a conciliatory tone of voice which could dilute your assertive words and message.

FIND YOUR INNER TODDLER

Think about children and how easily they say no. They're in touch with their needs and feelings, moment by moment. We were all toddlers once. We were all born assertive. If you have spent a lot of time putting other people's needs before your own, you may have lost sight of what really matters to you. You may find yourself answering 'I don't mind' or 'it doesn't matter to me' when you are trying to make decisions at work or at home. You can't ask for what you want if you don't really know what that is. To discover what you need, get in touch with your inner toddler and ask yourself:

- What do I need to feel happy and fulfilled?
- What would I love to do?
- How do I feel right now – physically and emotionally?
- Complete this sentence: I want...
- Complete this sentence: I don't want...
- If you dare, shout out 'no!' at the top of your voice and stamp your feet.

Being assertive improves our self-esteem and confidence. It is not about aggression, but about knowing what we want and being treated with respect.

BE COMPASSIONATE WITH YOURSELF

Renowned meditation teacher Tara Brach shows us how to treat ourselves with a little tenderness.

We all get lost in the dense forest of our lives, entangled in incessant worry, in judgements of others and in our busy striving to meet demands. When we're caught up in that thicket, it's easy to lose sight of what matters most. We forget how much we long to be kind and open-hearted,' says Brach, author of *Radical Compassion*. Here, she shares a four-step process to find our way back to ourselves, using the acronym 'RAIN':

1. Recognize When you are triggered by a thought that makes you anxious or irritable, or you find yourself reacting instead of responding, try to notice the sensations you feel and your emotions. Become an observer of your reactions; for example, a loved one is trying to get your attention and you're snappy – and that makes you feel guilty.

2. Allow Pause for a moment and let yourself feel what you're feeling, be it guilt, worry or anxiety. You're not saying that these feelings are positive ones, simply that they are present in the here and now.

3. Investigate Now, gently and with kindness, ask: 'What's going on?' Do you feel that if you don't get your work done, you will fail? Do you feel that you are failing your loved one for not giving them your attention? Is that feeling of failure familiar? Where do you experience it in your body?

4. Nurture Ask yourself: 'What do I need?' Imagine someone you trust is giving you a hug. Spend as much time as you need, offering the care you require inwardly. 'Calling on the most wise and compassionate part of your being, you might offer yourself a loving message,' says Brach.

THE POWER OF SMALL TALK

People disparage small talk as superficial, but it is actually the foundation of some of our biggest conversations, and a skill we can all master.

We mock small talk – even the name is pejorative. People dismiss it as lightweight and insubstantial, but that's like dismissing the fuel on which aircraft run as unimportant. Small talk is the oil that lubricates 'big talk'. Without it, there would be no great romances, friendships, business deals or successful diplomatic negotiations.

LET ME SUSS YOU OUT

'Small talk can be a frivolous end in itself or the warm-up act to a big conversation,' says Catherine Blyth, author of *The Art of Conversation*. 'It is the phase of familiarizing yourself with somebody, exchanging light topics, gauging one another's point of view and sense of humour and mapping your common ground... Then you can dig deeper.'

If you dread the thought of someone judging you for not saying something earth-shattering, remember that most people will be glad you've broken the ice. When they ask how many children you have, they are just keen to show that they're friendly and interested.

The mistress of small talk was Queen Elizabeth II. How many dignitaries did she put at ease by finding a way into a conversation? How many of those people were visiting on important state business? Small talk is as much for matters of state as it is for passing time at the bus stop.

'The most serious discussions must begin somewhere,' says Blyth. 'Lead small talk successfully and you are at an advantage.

Asking simple questions can spark long and rich discussions – and small talk gets easier with practice. Stay positive and try to ask open-ended questions.

The initial mood influences the tenor of the interaction. Jokes, enquiries, smiles and frowns set a tone and are powerful. They yield clues about a person's mindset and intentions, and can subvert them too.'

Small talk can boost your mood too. In a study at the University of British Columbia, participants were asked to seek an interaction with a barista in a coffee shop, while others were told to keep their exchanges efficient. The results revealed that those who chatted reported more positive emotions, suggesting that interactions with others, however peripheral they are to our lives, are essential for our wellbeing.

So, the next time a person makes a remark about the weather, don't dismiss it as meaningless – small talk puts the world to rights as much as big talk.

CHATTY PARTY PLAN

AUTHOR CATHERINE BLYTH gives the following tips on how to oil the wheels of conversation at a social gathering.

Get the ball rolling
Introduce yourself and start with a non-confrontational exchange. Think of potential topics beforehand, then scatter them lightly to see which ones engage the other person.

Be curious
Listen carefully, ask questions and build on what the other person says in response to your opening gambit. Try to establish what interests them and encourage them to tell you more. Being interested in someone is the best way to find out what is interesting about them.

Use body language
Give the person your full attention and don't look over their shoulder while you are conversing! Nod, smile and show that you are interested in them. Nothing kills a conversations faster than appearing bored.

Move it along
Once you've established common ground, you might want to offer your opinions or feelings. Don't overshare, but a simple acknowledgement that you find parties nerve-racking allows the other person to reveal something about themselves in exchange. Remember to respect boundaries. Some people are happy to share details about their lives from the outset, while others are more reserved.

HEALTHY BODY, HEALTHY MIND

The care we give to our bodies has a huge effect on our state of mind, from making sure we get good sleep and wholesome nutrition to stress-busting exercises and memory-boosting mind techniques. Treat your body well and your mind will thank you for it.

EXERCISE FOR HAPPINESS

Getting a sweat on not only improves your health, but it can also help to boost your mood. Here's how the latest science suggests you reap the feel-good rewards.

Think back to the moments after your last workout and remember how you felt. Were you happier and more energized than your pre-workout self? Did you feel as though you could take on the world? These kind of mental health benefits are welcome bonuses to those who exercise, but could you work out solely to boost your mood? While happiness is a subjective concept, the latest science suggests that how physically active you are is a good indicator of your emotional state. Case in point – one study in the journal *BMC Public Health* revealed that being very active increased the odds of being happy by an impressive 52 per cent. Another study from Korea showed that participants who exercised for 30 minutes a day, five times per week, were more likely to be happy than those who were sedentary, and 2020 data reported that inactive folk felt bad, on average, for 18 more days every year than those who exercised. The evidence supporting exercise as a happiness remedy is stacking high.

ENHANCE YOUR MOOD HORMONES
There are some obvious reasons for these results – people who stay physically active produce disease-fighting antibodies that boost general health, a key component of happiness – but mood-enhancing hormones also play a role. 'Exercise is well known to cause the release

of endorphins, serotonin, dopamine, and testosterone,' says Dr Deborah Lee, from online doctor and pharmacy service Dr Fox Pharmacy (doctorfox.co.uk). 'Endorphins and dopamine induce a pleasure sensation, giving you a high. Serotonin is a neurotransmitter which helps control appetite and sleep, and helps you become calm and relaxed. And testosterone is needed for both men and women to build muscle, help regulate the metabolism and fire up libido. 'Exercise can quash stress, too – although physical activity increases levels of stress hormones such as cortisol and adrenaline initially, research suggests these levels decrease later on. 'Exercise helps to redress the [hormonal] balance,' adds Dr Lee. 'Because the serotonin and dopamine released when exercising overwhelm adrenaline and cortisol, they help to calm your overactive stress response.'

FEELING ON EDGE?

During stressful times such as the COVID-19 pandemic, exercise can cut through the chaos by offering brain-boosting rewards. 'Neuroscience studies show that some parts of the brain, such as the amygdala and hippocampus, play a role in the control of happiness,' explains Dr Joel Chidley, lecturer in sport, outdoor and exercise science at the University of Derby. 'We know that exercise can protect the amygdala and hippocampus against Alzheimer's disease-related degeneration, so it's possible to speculate that it may also influence happiness through activity in these brain regions.'

BOUNCE BACK STRONGER

But there's more to happiness than your body's chemical response – experts are quick to point out that other factors influence our wellbeing, such as our social interactions, financial security and the way in which we deal with stress. Fortunately, exercise makes it easier to bounce back from so many of these setbacks, which can go a long way to increasing your sense of wellness. 'Feeling physically strong helps you to feel

mentally strong,' agrees Lydia Kimmerling, master life coach. 'In 2020, I began training for a half Iron Man and my intention was purely to strengthen my resilience. The race was cancelled a few weeks before, however the months of training had taught me a lot about myself and what I was capable of.'

THE CATCH?

The exercise you choose matters. Scientists have noticed that different activities have different impacts on emotional wellbeing – for example, sports which involve an element of socializing, such as team sports, have a more positive effect on mental health than solitary forms of activity (see panel opposite for more mood boosters). And if you don't feel ready to sign up for a club yet, online group classes and challenges are a great place to start. 'You don't need to overthink it,' adds Kimmerling. 'It's usually just a case of getting to the first class or session which is the hardest, then by using exercise as a starting point, you'll bypass your mental state and use your physical state to change your emotional state.'

GOOD FOR MENTAL HEALTH

Exercise is clearly good for your mental health, but how much should you be doing to feel happier right now? 'As little as 10 minutes per week may greatly increase your odds of being happy,' reports Dr Chidley. Little and often is key here, as be warned: you can have too much of a good thing. 'While the benefits seem to continue to increase with greater levels of exercise (at least up to the recommended 150 minutes, which can be accumulated throughout the week), there is some evidence of a plateau, with no difference in happiness levels between groups of individuals that completed 150 minutes of weekly activity and those that completed 300 minutes per week.' Indeed, excessive amounts of exercise have even been linked to over-training syndrome, which has been found to cause low mood and sometimes depression.

The good news is that you don't have to exercise hard to feel your mood improve. 'Just putting on your favourite song and dancing around the room is enough to help you feel happier,' says Kimmerling. 'Just find something that you love, then you can shift your mindset so that moving your body becomes something you give to yourself because it helps you to feel good.' And while outdoor exercise has been linked to improvements in happiness, thanks to our innate need to be among nature, Dr Chidley suggests that lighter forms of indoor activity count too: 'Randomized controlled trials have demonstrated that aerobic exercise and stretching/balancing exercises are equally effective in improving happiness. It appears that various intensities are beneficial, whether light, moderate or hard.

MOOD-BOOSTING MOVES

NEED TO SWEAT YOUR WAY out of a mood funk? Here are some of the best forms of exercise to balance your emotions:

RUNNING – You surely know that jogging triggers the body to release the endorphins that lead to a 'runner's high', but one study by Glasgow Caledonian University showed that the sense of community that runners got from apps such as Strava also had a positive impact.

YOGA – Mindful exercise has long been linked to a calmer state of mind, and studies show that levels of the brain's gamma-aminobutyric acid (GABA, which is linked to lower levels of depression) spike after just a single hour of yoga.

DANCE – There's a reason why dancers have 'happy feet' – data show that dancing may not only initiate a bigger release of endorphins than other forms of exercise, but it also prompts an emotional release that can help participants to let go of pent-up feelings.

POWER UP YOUR MOOD!

Whether your goal is to feel happier, improve your mental focus or alleviate stress and feel calmer, there are foods that can tick all of those boxes. You really are what you eat!

Uncertainty, fear and anxiety caused by ongoing stress can place its toll on our bodies, health and mood. However, the good news is that our diet and lifestyle can have a profound effect on our mood, motivation and resilience. Research is revealing how low mood, anxiety and depression are linked to a number of underlying factors, including inflammation, blood sugar imbalances, oxidative stress, poor methylation, and gut and hormone imbalances. These can all impact the balance of neurotransmitters (such as GABA, dopamine and serotonin) that affect how we think and feel.

KEY NUTRIENTS

By eating the right foods, you provide your body with the key nutrients needed to produce the brain chemicals that give you a natural lift. Of particular importance are amino acids from protein-rich foods. Without sufficient protein in your diet, your mood is likely to suffer. Dopamine, for example, which creates pleasure and keeps us motivated, is made from the amino acids tyrosine and phenylalanine. Serotonin requires the amino acid tryptophan, and GABA can be made from glutamine. The production of neurotransmitters is also dependent on sufficient levels of certain vitamins and minerals, including magnesium, copper, zinc, B vitamins and folate. There are other important nutrients to support healthy mood, too. For example, insufficient levels of vitamin D, phospholipids (a group of fats) and omega 3 fats can also impact on how we think and feel. In the same way, certain food choices can have a negative effect on mood. We have all experienced that sugar high followed by an energy crash after raiding the cookie jar. Sugar highs

and lows are just one way food can affect our mood. Skipping meals or not eating enough can also result in falling blood sugar levels, which can make us feel 'hangry' and irritable. Whether you are looking to reduce stress or boost energy and mood, over the next few pages we reveal some of the top foods and drinks that will help you feel calmer and happier.

DEFLATE STRESS

Anxiety, nervousness and fear are often linked to lower levels of the neurotransmitter GABA and excess levels of stress hormones, such as cortisol. Try the following foods...

Dark chocolate boosts feel-good hormones while suppressing the stress hormone cortisol.

Dark chocolate – There are over 300 naturally occurring chemicals in chocolate, and some of them, such as phenylethylamine, can boost our mood. Dark chocolate and cocoa powder are rich in magnesium, which helps to relax our nervous system and calm the mind. Stress robs the body of magnesium, but the body must have magnesium to respond effectively to stress. Snack on a couple of squares of dark chocolate or make your own chocolate energy balls.

Beans – Butterbeans, kidney beans, haricot and other beans contain the nutrient inositol, which has been shown to reduce worry and anxiety, as well as improve mood. Beans also provide protein and fibre, making them ideal for stabilizing blood sugar levels and keeping energy levels high. Why not try them tossed into salads or added to a warming soup or stew?

Chamomile tea is made from dried chamomile flowers. A cup before bedtime aids relaxation.

Chamomile – The chamomile plant contains a natural compound called apigenin, which has been found to reduce anxiety. Used as a herbal infusion, it is ideal as a warming evening drink to help you unwind.

Yogurt – Fermented foods, such as yogurt, kefir and sauerkraut, contain a range of beneficial gut-loving bacteria. The influence of our gut bacteria on mental health is gaining more attention in research, with studies showing they can help improve resilience and reduce anxiety. Try a bowl of Greek yogurt with berries for a sweet treat.

FOCUS AND MOTIVATION

Here are some choices to improve concentration...

Green tea – Contains a combination of caffeine and the amino acid L-theanine, which helps to increase certain neurotransmitters in the brain, such as GABA, improving your focus and concentration.

Eggs – The protein in eggs can significantly boost your levels of tryptophan and tyrosine – the building blocks for serotonin and dopamine. Dopamine is a key brain chemical that can improve motivation, productivity and focus. Eggs also provide the nutrient choline, which supports overall brain function and memory.

Avocado – Rich in monounsaturated fats which are known to lower inflammation (inflammation can disrupt levels of mood-boosting neurotransmitters). Avocados also provide tyrosine, an amino acid that helps the body produce dopamine.

Almonds – Contain a wealth of B vitamins and magnesium needed for production of brain chemicals. They are perfect as a healthy snack.

As well as helping to reduce inflammation, avocados contain vitamins C and B6, which lower stress, and potassium, which decreases blood pressure.

MOOD BOOST

If you're just feeling a little flat, here are some additional foods to perk up your mood...

Turmeric – Curcumin, one of the active compounds in turmeric, has been shown in studies to ease depression and boost mood. This may be due to its anti-inflammatory properties, because inflammation has been linked to depression. While absorption of curcumin from turmeric is limited, you can increase this by adding black pepper and a little oil when using. Try adding turmeric to soups and curries.

Chicken and turkey – These protein-packed foods are rich in tryptophan, which the body uses to make mood-boosting serotonin. Lean poultry also contains the amino acid tyrosine, which is needed to make mood-boosting dopamine. Chicken and turkey also contain B vitamins, including B12, which has been shown to help to fight depression.

Mushrooms are a natural source of vitamin D. Good varieties to try are maitake, morel, chanterelle, oyster and shiitake.

Salmon – Omega 3 rich foods, such as salmon, trout, sardines and mackerel, are well known brain foods. Low levels have been linked to increased anxiety and depression. Try to increase your intake of oily fish to two to three times a week, to really boost your levels.

Mushrooms – One of the few natural plant sources of vitamin D. Deficiencies in vitamin D have been associated with low mood and depression. Other food sources of vitamin D include oily fish, egg yolks and liver.

ENERGY LIFT

Struggling to keep going through the day? Here are some healthy energy boosters...

Berries – Loaded with antioxidants, berries are naturally sweet yet low in sugar and packed with fibre, to help keep energy levels high.

Bananas – These contain the amino acid tryptophan, as well as various nutrients, such as B6, which help convert tryptophan into the mood-boosting serotonin.

Coconut water – This is an excellent hydrating choice providing electrolytes like potassium and magnesium, plus some carbohydrate to give you a natural boost.

Oats – With their combination of slow-releasing carbohydrates and protein plus energy-boosting nutrients (such as B vitamins, iron, manganese and magnesium), oats are the perfect choice for boosting energy.

DON'T FORGET EXERCISE

LIFESTYLE CHANGES including exercise are just as important when it comes to improving mood. Aerobic exercise, yoga, resistance training and a combination of these have been reported to reduce depression symptoms. Exercise appears to increase serotonin, dopamine, brain-derived neurotrophic factor, norepinephrine and endorphins — all brain chemicals that have been associated with improved mood and mental health. So choose a form of exercise you like and enjoy the many benefits.

Darker berries are usually higher in natural antioxidants than lighter berries. They help to reduce inflammation and fatigue.

HOW TO KEEP YOUR BRAIN IN SHAPE

One of the world's top brain surgeons Dr Rahul Jandial gives the following lifestyle tips for keeping your mind and memory sharp well into old age.

Who better to look to for advice on keeping your body's most complex organ in tip-top shape than a brain surgeon? Alongside his own professional experience, Dr Rahul Jandial spent a decade looking at research for his book, *Life Lessons from a Brain Surgeon*, which busts common brain health myths and is packed with handy hacks for improved memory and cognition. For Dr Jandial, the physical brain is inextricably linked to mood and emotions, and one of the things that can affect both is sleep. 'We know [prolonged] lack of sleep affects everything. It can cause heart disease and other metabolic issues and is linked with mental health issues and Alzheimer's. But another thing people don't often talk about is how it can change your mood and emotional regulation,' says Dr Jandial. 'You're more sensitive, grumpy and more likely to feel hurt.'

He also looks at how emotions, as well as the more functional aspects of the brain such as memory, can both be symptoms of declining brain health – often evident with dementia. 'People with dementia don't just get lost and forget things. They're frustrated, upset, emotional, labile. Mood and memory are linked.'

LET THERE BE (LESS) LIGHT!

Although we think of sleep as a restful time, your brain is extremely active during slumber as it does its housekeeping, 'deleting all the [unnecessary] stimulation you had throughout the day' and locking in the important stuff, he says.

However, there are lots of myths around sleep, plus, what works for one person may not work for the next. Where the science is very clear, though, is on the role of light and dark. 'Two years ago, the Nobel Prize was given for figuring this out. The rotation of the earth, switching from dark to light, affects everything on the planet, from plants to animals to us, and the most important thing about sleep is light management,' says Dr Jandial.

Traditionally, dimming daylight would signal to your brain to start winding down, preparing you for slumber. But with so much artificial light in our environments now, many people are out of synch with natural light-dark cycles. 'The simplest advice is to start dimming the lights around 7–8 pm. That will set off the natural triggers to initiate sleep,' he says. This includes the lighting in your home, as well as your TV, laptop screens, tablets and phones.

BREATHE DEEPLY

Do your thoughts keep wandering when you try to meditate? It turns out that's OK, as it's your breathing that's the most important factor. This has been studied through experiments involving opening people's skulls and inserting grids on their brains, giving researchers a 'live feed' of activity! 'When asked to do controlled deep breathing – 3 seconds in, hold, 3 seconds out – the researchers found that regardless of what the participants were thinking, it changed the electrical flows within those people's brains,' says Dr Jandial.

'Controlled breathing is your built-in tranquility mode, triggering the release of chemicals that have an instant calming effect.' It's something he recommends weaving into everyday life. 'Whether that's 5 minutes before you get home because you're frustrated, or 5 minutes because you've been fighting with your partner, these results happen within minutes – you don't need hours, or to go to a silent retreat.'

TRAIN YOUR BRAIN

Memory is often described as a muscle that can be trained – so does this mean reliance on modern technology is harming our future brain health? Dr Jandial doesn't think it's as simplistic as that. Plus, some types of memory do naturally decrease with age – such as the ability to remember names, and where you put your keys. 'Our phones are going to help us with those things, they're our allies,' he says.

But there's plenty you can do to 'train' your memory and help stay sharp. 'Your frontal lobe is excellent at what's called "working memory" or as I prefer to call it, the "multi-tasking" or "juggling memory". This is the one we all ought to work on,' he says.

Although multi-tasking gets a bad rap, Dr Jandial says it's how effectively you do it that counts, and that juggling without dropping any balls is the best kind of memory practice there is. You can weave training tricks into your day-to-day routine. 'For example, try to remember what's on your calendar or to-do list before you look at it. Or look at your route before setting off somewhere, then see how far you can get without having to check the map again. That's the memory that's going to keep you effective at work and life.'

MOVE YOUR BODY

Exercise has endless benefits for the brain, starting with simply keeping up its vital blood supply. 'The brain is flesh and needs to be irrigated as much as any other part of the body — more than other parts of the body, in fact, because it's only 5 kg (11 lb) but gets 20 per cent of the body's blood flow. It's an energy hog! And if you have clogged arteries, you'll have swathes of brain wither inside your skull. This is essentially what happens with vascular dementia, which occurs due to restricted blood flow to the brain.'

Physical activity also enables you to activate your own 'internal pharmacy', says Dr Jandial, triggering the release of feel-good chemicals including dopamine and serotonin, which play a huge role in mental health. And it doesn't actually take much exercise to reap the benefits. 'These [chemicals] are not only released if you be become a marathon runner. They're released if you simply go from sitting around to standing and walking more,' he says. 'Regularly going for brisk 30-minute daily walks has been found to provide around an 80 per cent health boost from these feel-good chemicals, while a super fitness fanatic may be getting 90 per cent.' Time to lace up those walking boots...

SORTING YOUR SLEEP

Sleep is essential for a healthy state of mind. Here's how to make sure you're getting enough...

Create darkness

To enjoy quality sleep, it's best to be in complete darkness. Although your eyes might be closed, they will still pick up on light changes if the room isn't completely dark, which can keep your brain from fully relaxing into deep sleep or wake you up too soon. Try using a blackout curtain or an eye mask if you live somewhere with street lights outside.

Avoid EMFs

Your computer, tablet, phone and Wi-Fi router produce an electromagnetic field (EMF). This field, although it can be small, can interrupt brain signaling and disturb the quality of your sleep. Try to remove all computers, phones and electrical equipment from your bedroom and turn off your router at night, even if it's in a different room.

Cut the sound

Along with light, sound can keep your brain over-stimulated. Your danger monitoring system can interpret innocent sounds such as a car driving past or a dog barking as danger and wake you up, even temporarily. And even short wake breaks in the night can affect your repair and recovery. Wear ear plugs that cut out all or most noise if you find you can't switch off or that sounds keep disturbing you.

Relax your sympathetic nervous system

Looking at your computer, TV or phone late at night over-stimulates your brain, making you more hyper-alert – especially if you watch crime dramas or other shows that get your heart racing. This makes it much harder to relax and sleep. It's advisable to turn off all your computers and put your phone on silent or flight mode from 8 pm at the latest, and wear red or orange glasses when you watch TV so that the blue light doesn't interfere with your melatonin production, which is the hormone that helps you fall asleep. Blue light is what stops its production, as your body thinks it's daytime.

Feel good before bed

The stress of the day or any long-term stress can hinder sleep. Try writing down five positives from your day, such as things you are grateful for, no matter how small. This focuses your mind on good experiences, which sets you up for better sleep.

It's also good to let go of any irritations, especially towards others. If, for example, someone has annoyed you, you can say in your head: 'I forgive that person and release any ill feeling towards them.' Anger and frustration towards others only affects you negatively, not the other person, so it's best to release it if you can.

Emotional Freedom Technique (tapping) helps with this. Look up 'Tap with Brad' on YouTube to find a tapping sequence for pretty much every emotion and situation.

LOST IN MUSIC

No matter what your mood, allow music to bring you into the present moment with these simple steps towards mindful meditation...

1. Listen to a song that speaks to your emotions. Whether that means listening to Christmas carols, your favourite tunes from school or one of Tchaikovsky's symphonies, use music to engage your ears and awaken joyous memories.

2. Unleash your inner child and give yourself permission to finally learn that instrument you've had your eye on since you were young. Experiment with your own melodies and enjoy the sound created by your own two hands.

3. Celebrate the feelings evoked by your music, whether you're the musician or the listener. Turn up the volume on your sound system and pay close attention to the way the beats, instruments, voices and lyrics interact with your own thoughts.

HOW TO DITCH COMFORT EATING

Break free from the emotional eating cycle and discover how to carve out a healthy relationship with food.

Food has the power to induce feelings of happiness, but when we are tempted to eat for reasons other than to quell hunger, it can cause a rollercoaster of negative health effects. A disconnect between our emotions and our eating habits can also result in overeating. This is because eating is a subconscious act, and we often don't stop and think why we are reaching for certain foods.

So, why are our brains wired to seek out sweet foods? 'Sugar provides us with a natural high,' says Dr Elena Touroni, a consultant psychologist and co-founder of The Chelsea Psychology Clinic (thechelseapsychologyclinic.com). 'We're conditioned from an early age to comfort ourselves with sweet foods. They give us a physiological high, so it can easily make up part of a rehearsed strategy for dealing with difficult feelings.' There is a chemical process, too. Neurons in the brain release the reward neurotransmitter dopamine in response to eating sugar, from which you experience pleasure. You consume more in order to get the same pleasure hit. Over time, your brain's dopamine system builds up tolerance, which creates a cycle of excess consumption to try to fulfil unrelenting cravings.

To get this system back in check, it's important to pinpoint food triggers and look to means other than food in order to feel satisfied. Here we share our top ways to beat cravings...

1. FOCUS ON THE JOURNEY

The journey to healthy eating is a marathon and not a sprint, so aim to make manageable changes that you can stick to. Instead of focusing on deprivation, think about how you can make your diet better. This might mean loading up on an extra portion of vegetables at mealtimes, or making sure that you start the day with a healthy breakfast.

2. START WITH SIMPLE SWAPS

Making healthy swaps is an easy way to cut down on sugar and fat, and doesn't mean you have to compromise on flavour. UK government guidelines state that adults should consume no more than 30 g (1 oz) of free sugars (found in foods such as biscuits and cakes) per day. This works out as seven sugar cubes – but the less sugar you consume, the better, so ideally aim for half this amount. Replace white sugar with a small amount of honey or maple syrup, have brown rice, bread and pasta instead of white versions, and oat cakes instead of biscuits. Replace high-sugar fruits like grapes for low-sugar apples and pears.

3. SNACK SMART

Eating little and often will help to keep your blood sugar levels even. This means keeping lots of nutritious snacks on hand so that you don't cave into unhealthy cravings the moment hunger strikes. If you work from home, you might be tempted to snack more than you usually would, so make sure you always have healthy options available for a mid-morning and mid-afternoon snack. Guacamole with crudités or a banana topped with almond butter are good options to keep those all-important blood sugar levels stable.

4. GET A HEALTHY MINDSET

A healthy mindset will help you to follow a balanced diet, so don't ban any food from your diet. Allow yourself the occasional treat to help you strengthen your resolve to stick to a more nutritious diet. This could mean having your favourite ice cream or chocolate once a week, but limiting portion size.

5. AVOID SWEETENERS

Artificial sweeteners take the place of traditional sugar in foods such as low-fat yogurts or diet drinks, but research suggests that consuming sweeteners can stimulate the hunger cycle so that you actually eat more. Read food labels and avoid any pre-packaged foods that are made with artificial sweeteners.

6. EAT TRYPTOPHAN FOODS

Tryptophan is an amino acid and co-factor in the production of the feel-good chemical messenger serotonin, which helps to stabilize mood. Cheese, turkey and nuts are all tryptophan-rich foods.

7. KEEP YOUR GUT HEALTHY

A high-fibre diet which contains wholegrains along with probiotic-rich foods including sauerkraut, kefir and yogurt will help to fuel healthy gut bacteria. Digestive microflora plays a role in serotonin levels through the gut-brain axis, so it's important to keep beneficial bacteria flourishing. High-fibre foods include fruit and veg, beans, legumes, bread, grains and nuts. Berries and apples are high-fibre choices and therefore filling.

8. UPGRADE YOUR SLEEP

Bad sleep habits can stimulate food cravings, so get your bedtime routine in check. One night of poor sleep can disrupt the function of your cerebrum – the area of the brain responsible for complex decision-making, which could result in next-day cravings. Poor sleep disrupts levels of the appetite hormones leptin and ghrelin, while increasing levels of the stress hormone cortisol. All of these can stimulate your appetite, meaning you eat more than usual after a bad night's sleep. Reducing technology use at least an hour before bed, having a bath and sipping a calming tea can all help you to sleep better.

Bad sleep habits can stimulate food cravings, so try to get your bedtime routine in check.

9. KEEP A JOURNAL

Identify any triggers for emotional eating to create a healthier relationship with food.
Logging your daily food intake will allow you to tailor your diet to your needs and pinpoint patterns and habits in order to get the most out of your mealtimes.

HEALTHY GUT, HEALTHY MIND

The latest scientific research suggests that many diseases of the mind might originate in the gut. If so, could treating your microbiome be the way to a healthier state of mind?

You might consider conditions such as depression and anxiety purely brain-based issues, but studies suggest that the gut may have an important role to play. 'We are increasingly finding out more about the gut microbiome in relation to health and disease,' says Professor Glenn Gibson, head of Food Microbial Sciences at the University of Reading. 'The connection that the gut could be involved in migraine and schizophrenia was first made in the 1800s. This was not taken seriously at the time. But, we now know that the gut microbiome is central to many disorders. These include cognitive issues, anxiety, depression, migraines, autism, dementia, and Parkinson's disease.'

'It is clear that that gut bacteria produce chemicals that can have both positive and negative effects on the brain (neurotransmitters),' says Professor Gibson. 'These are transmitted via the vagus nerve that connects the brain and gut. The key is finding out which bacteria produce which neurochemical and how it then becomes involved in the issue.'

CROSSING INTO YOUR BRAIN

'The connection between the gut and brain is real, it's powerful and it may revolutionize medicine as we know it,' says Caltech microbiologist Sarkis Mazmanian. 'Inside our brain is a coating called the blood-brain barrier. This is like a gate that selectively allows good molecules (neurotransmitters, hormones and nutrients) to pass freely, but prevents the entry of bad molecules (e.g. toxins) that are harmful to the brain.'

Yet despite this, the gut and brain are in constant communication, through incoming or outgoing nerves, or small molecules that pass through the blood-brain barrier. These signals tell you about your mood, cognition, hunger and other responses. And it turns out these molecules that cross the blood-brain barrier are created by the trillions of bacteria that make up your microbiome, most of which are in your gut.

'The gut absorbs nutrients from food, and also from the many thousands of molecules from bacteria that can reach all corners of our bodies, including our brain,' says Mazmanian. 'By fixing problems in our gut this may naturally fix issues in the brain associated with different diseases. The future of medicine may include the concept of "drugs from bugs", meaning some day you may go to the doctor and be prescribed a pill with live bacteria inside as a remedy.'

FIVE TIPS TO KEEP YOUR GUT HEALTHY

DR RANGAN CHATTERJEE, author of *Feel Better In Five* (drchatterjee.com), is one of many doctors interested in gut health. 'Over the past 5 to 10 years we've started to realize that the health of our gut doesn't only affect digestion, it also affects overall health and wellbeing,' he says. Follow his tips for good gut health.

- Remove things from your diet that are damaging your gut bacteria, such as highly processed foods, additives and sweeteners.

- Eat a variety of plant foods; aim to eat at least five differently coloured fruits and vegetables a day. If you really want to ramp it up, aim to eat 26 different plant foods in any given month.

- Eat all of your food in a 12-hour window. For example, if you have breakfast at

7 am, have your last meal by 7 pm. when you give your gut bugs a break from your food intake, certain populations of bacteria start to thrive. Eating this way is also associated with better immune system control, better immune system function and even losing weight.

- Eat some fermented (probiotic) foods such as kefir, kimchi and sauerkraut. These foods introduce beneficial bacteria into your gut.

- Eat prebiotic foods such as bananas, asparagus, Jerusalem artichoke, garlic, onion, leeks, chicory root and dandelion greens, as the fibres in these foods encourage beneficial bacteria in your gut to thrive. (If you find these make you feel bloated and uncomfortable, you may have a bacterial imbalance, so look into the FODMAP diet).

HEALING YOGA

More than just a physical workout, yoga calms and focuses the mind, bringing about a host of benefits – from easing pain to alleviating stress.

In the West, yoga is often seen simply as a way to stretch and condition the body. But this ancient practice is so much more than that. Yoga is a complete system of exercise, breathing, meditation and relaxation that helps you deal with the demands of life. Far from just a feel-good workout, it has a host of clinically proven physical and mental benefits, from easing aches and pains and reducing blood pressure to alleviating insomnia, depression and stress.

ROOTS AND EVOLUTION

Yoga originated around 5000 BC from an ancient Indian philosophy called Vedanta, which emphasized the connection between mind and body. The word 'yoga' is derived from the Sanskrit word 'yuj', which means 'yoke' or 'union'. This is because over time, doing yoga helps connect your body and mind, bringing you closer to understanding yourself. In today's busy world, yoga can give you the space to breathe and reconnect to your body's needs.

Around 2,500 years ago in India, an author and sage named Patañjali wrote the first real practical yoga guide – a book called *The Yoga Sutras*. Patañjali defined yoga with the Sanskrit phrase 'citti-vrtti-nirohdah', which translates as 'the cessation of the turnings of the mind'. Even today, the basic definition of yoga has changed little. It's ultimately about stilling the chatter in your mind through focus – whether that is on your alignment and breath when doing postures, or on a mantra, your breath or an object during a breathing exercise or meditation.

In the 20th century, teachers from India developed different forms of hatha yoga. B.K.S. Iyengar created the structured Iyengar form, while Sri K. Pattabhi Jois created the dynamic ashtanga style. In the second half of the century, yoga began to flourish in the West, as enthusiasts travelled to India and brought their knowledge back home. Now, there are many hybrids, from hot yoga to dynamic yoga. But certain elements are always present: focus, centering and a returning to our inner selves and a more peaceful state.

YOGA AND YOU

While the human mind tends to focus on the past or future, the body exists only in the present. Coming back to your body through yoga postures brings your mind back to the present moment. And for that moment, your worries drop away – you're fully connected to your body. The more you practise, the stronger your body will become and the more powerfully connected you will feel to your body. The more connected to your body you feel, the less you'll be susceptible to the stresses and strains of everyday life. A calm mind, stronger body and glowing skin are just some of the benefits you'll reap from regular practice.

THE FIVE PILLARS

The main aim of yoga is to bring your body and all its cravings, passions, worries and urges under the control of your mind. Indian sage Patañjali defined yoga through methods such as controlling your breath and holding your body in steady poses – now known as hatha yoga. Today, yoga has evolved into many modern-day hybrids – from the physically challenging ashtanga and Bikram yoga to restorative yin and meditative raja yoga. But the basic principles of hatha yoga remain the same and can be broken down into five essential principles that create a total conditioning system for your body.

1. Exercise

In yoga, exercise takes the form of 'asanas', or postures, which lubricate, strengthen, stretch and tone your body. Although they can be demanding, yoga asanas are different from other forms of exercise as

they incorporate both challenge and recovery. Rather than only focusing on dramatically expending energy, yoga focuses on conserving and renewing your energy, so that after each session you'll feel refreshed and energized.

2. Breathing

Correct breathing deepens your yoga practice and has a direct impact on your nervous system. A range of yogic breathing techniques, known as pranayama, can help calm, restore and energize your body and mind. Your breath links your body to your solar plexus, located deep in your navel, where potential energy is stored and created. The yoga breath helps release this energy for mental and physical restoration.

3. Relaxation

Yoga recognizes that proper, regular relaxation releases tension and allows you to make new energy, even when you're tired and overworked. Relaxation is therefore a central part of any yoga practice. The most powerfully restoring posture is Savasana, where you lie flat, face up, with your eyes closed. This is used at the end of yoga practice or in between demanding poses. According to yoga experts, it's among the most important of all postures as it's the time when your body assimilates the accumulated benefits of the preceding practice. Don't be tempted to skip it!

4. Meditation

Meditation and mindfulness – even a few minutes a day – are an essential part of yoga, because they help control, focus and refresh your mind. But don't worry, meditation doesn't have to mean sitting in the Lotus position for hours! Mindfulness meditation simply requires observing your thoughts as though they're clouds in the sky, shifting and changing. Or try the 'RAIN' meditation exercise on page 90. Your meditation can take place at the end of your yoga practice or for 10 minutes in the morning. You can even do it for a minute on the bus or train or between meetings. A little regular meditation done often is better than a lot, done sporadically.

5. Diet

Yoga philosophy recommends a diet of simple, natural foods that are easily digested, to promote good physical and mental health. Ideally vegetarian, a yogic diet should include fruit, vegetables, grains, leafy greens, dairy produce, pulses, nuts and seeds. Eating mindfully until you are only 80 per cent full is also recommended.

STRETCH AND RELAX

Try yoga to bring balance and harmony into your life.

'Stress causes a fight-or-flight response which, if present for too long, can cause other health problems such as poor sleep and IBS,' explains yoga teacher Hannah Barrett (hannahbarrettyoga.com). 'Yoga releases endorphins (happy hormones) and incorporates mindfulness and meditation – all shown to help reduce anxiety.' Indeed, one study reports that practising yoga can encourage the release of gamma-aminobutyric acid (GABA) in the brain, a calming neurotransmitter. And that's not all. 'By bringing attention to your breath and the movement of your body, you stimulate the parasympathetic nervous system (the rest and digest system),' adds Hannah. 'This allows muscles to relax, inflammatory levels to lower and the gut to digest food more efficiently.' Studies show that some yoga poses are more effective than others when it comes to dialling down anxiety levels, so try Hannah's sequences below to feel more relaxed.

ALTERNATE NOSTRIL BREATHING (NADI SHODHANA)
This technique helps to activate the parasympathetic nervous system and promote a sense of calm.
- Breathe consciously, staying aware of your breath throughout.
- Sit with a straight spine, in a comfortable cross-legged position and with your eyes closed.
- Tuck the index and middle fingers of your right hand into your palm and exhale fully to begin.
- Bring your right thumb to your face and use it to close your right nostril. Take a full, slow inhale through your left nostril.
- Close your left nostril with your ring finger, then simultaneously release your right nostril and exhale slowly. Take a full and slow inhale through your right nostril.
- Close your right nostril with your thumb, then release your left nostril and exhale slowly. This is one round. Repeat for 8–12 rounds.

CHILD'S POSE (BALASANA)

This helps to release tension in your back, neck and shoulders.

- Kneel on the floor with your big toes together and your knees about hip-width apart.
- Exhale and bend forwards from the hips, so that your torso rests between your thighs. Keep your spine extended.
- Stretch your arms forwards, feeling a stretch from your tailbone to your fingertips. Alternatively, bring your arms back and place your hands on the floor, alongside your torso with palms up. Relax the fronts of your shoulders toward the floor.
- Rest here for five slow breaths, or longer if required.

RESTORATIVE FISH POSE (MATSYASANA)

This pose helps to relieve tension in your neck and shoulders, opening your chest and allowing a deeper breath, which improves blood circulation.

- Place a pillow, bolster or block horizontal to the short edge of your mat, about a foot-and-a-half away from the back of the mat. If you would like to, place another pillow or block (for your head to rest on) at the back of the mat.
- Gently lie back over the prop pillow, bolster or block, bringing the bottom edge of it to just below the tips of your shoulder blades. Put the other prop under your head, if you desire.
- Relax your entire body and place your arms to the side or overhead – whichever is most comfortable. Stay here for 1–2 minutes or more.
- When exiting the pose, gently roll to one side and remove the props.

CAT COW (MARJARYASANA)

This move brings fluidity to the body, helping to open your chest and back, which can hold a lot of tension.

• Start in a table-top position – wrists under your shoulders, knees under your hips.

• Inhale into the cow pose by gazing forwards and arching your spine. Keep your neck long and chest forwards. Engage your core by drawing your navel in.

• Exhale into the cat pose by tucking your pelvis under and rounding your back. Relax your head and push into the ground with your hands, which will pull your shoulder blades away from your spine.

• Continue moving through the cow and cat poses for five full breaths.

FORWARD FOLD (UTTANASANA)

This helps to calm your mind and can relieve tension headaches. It stretches your lower back and hips.

- Exhale and slowly bend forward from the hips. Find length in your spine as you fold, bending your knees if required.
- Bring your palms or fingertips to the floor, onto blocks or to the backs of your ankles or shins.
- Press your feet into the floor and lift your hip bones, turning the top of your thighs slightly in. Squeeze your lower belly up and in, and let your head hang.
- Take five deep breaths or more. With each inhale, find a little more length in your torso and with each exhale, release a little more into the fold.

CONTRIBUTORS

Oliver Burkman

Lizzie Enfield

Anita Chauduri

Sally Brown

Julia Samuel

Ali Roff Farrar

Chloe Brotheridge

Malcolm Stern

Sarah Sellens

Larissa Chapman

Abi Jackson

Katy Sunnassee

Eva Gizowska

Rachel Tompkins